Essential Music Theory © 2022 by San Marco Publications. All rights reserved.

All right reserved. No part of this book may be reproduced in any form or by electronic or mechanical means including Information storage and retrieval systems without permission in writing from the author.

ISNB: 9781896499309

Contents

Lesson 1: **Pitch and Notation** — 1

Lesson 2: **Time** — 5

Lesson 3: **Major Scales** — 29

Lesson 4: **History 1** — 37

Review 1 — 40

Lesson 5: **Minor Scales** — 44

Lesson 6: **Intervals 1** — 54

Lesson 7: **Intervals 2** — 58

Lesson 8: **History 2** — 62

Review 2 — 67

Lesson 9: **Chords** — 69

Lesson 10: **Octave Transposition** — 80

Lesson 11: **Melody Writing** — 84

Lesson 12: **Form and Analysis** — 92

Lesson 13: **History 3** — 97

Review 3 — 99

Music Terms and Signs — 101

1
Pitch and Notation

Ledger Lines

Ledger lines are used to extend the range of the staff. Ledger lines are spaced the same distance vertically as the lines of the staff.

Figure 1.1

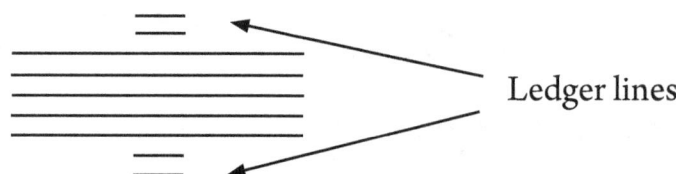

Ledger lines

Stems of all notes above and below the first ledger line must extend to the middle staff line (Figure 1.2).

Figure 1.2

middle line

In this level we will study notes up to four ledger lines above and below the staff. Figure 1.3 shows these ledger line notes on the treble staff.

Figure 1.3

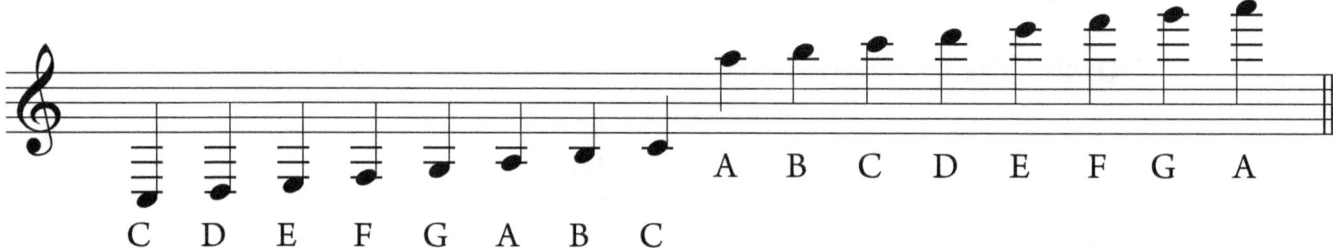

© San Marco Publications 2022

1. Write the following notes using ledger lines below the treble staff.

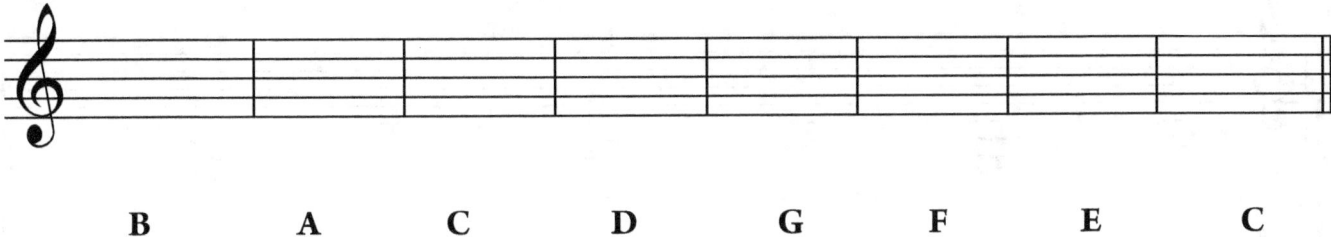

      B   A   C   D   G   F   E   C

2. Write the following notes using ledger lines above the treble staff.

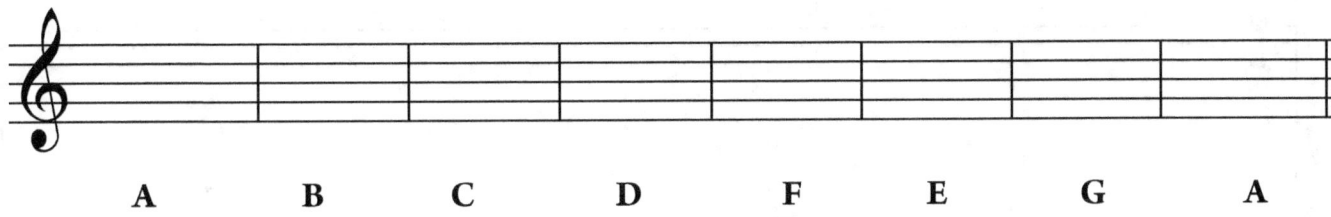

      A   B   C   D   F   E   G   A

Figure 1.4 shows the ledger line notes on the bass staff.

Figure 1.4

3. Write the following notes using ledger lines below the bass staff.

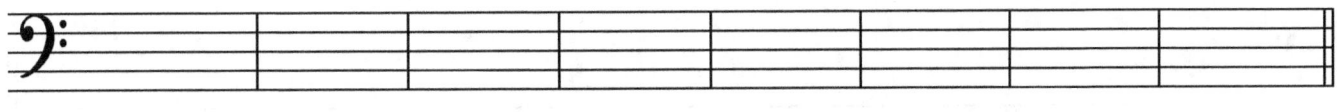

      A   B   D   C   E   G   F   E

4. Write the following notes using ledger lines above the bass staff.

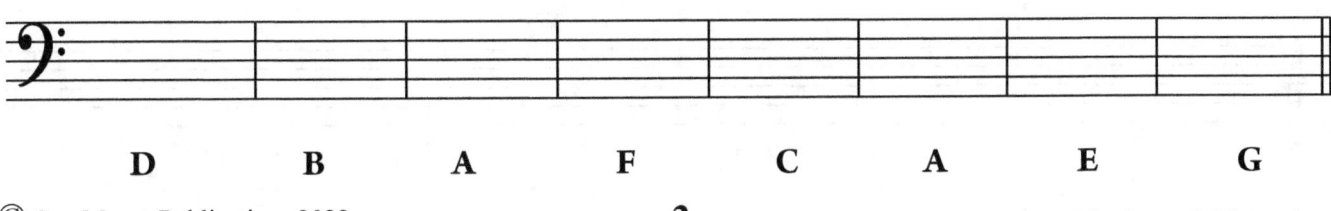

      D   B   A   F   C   A   E   G

© San Marco Publications 2022   Pitch and Notation

5. Name the following notes and then write them at the same pitch in the other clef.

6. Rewrite the following melodies in the other clef without changing the pitch.

Jean Sibelius
Symphony No. 3, III

Enharmonic Equivalents

Each black key on the keyboard has both a sharp name and a flat name. When notes have the same pitch but different names they are said to be *enharmonic equivalents*. Enharmonic basically means "same note different name". They are the same note, but they have different meanings. It's like the words there, their, and they're. They sound the same but mean something different. There are many reasons why we call some notes by alternate names, and we will learn more about that when we study scales and keys.

Figure 1.5 shows some of the enharmonic notes on the keyboard. Some of the white keys may have more than one name. B♯ is also C and B is also C♭. E♯ is also F and E is also F♭.

Figure 1.5

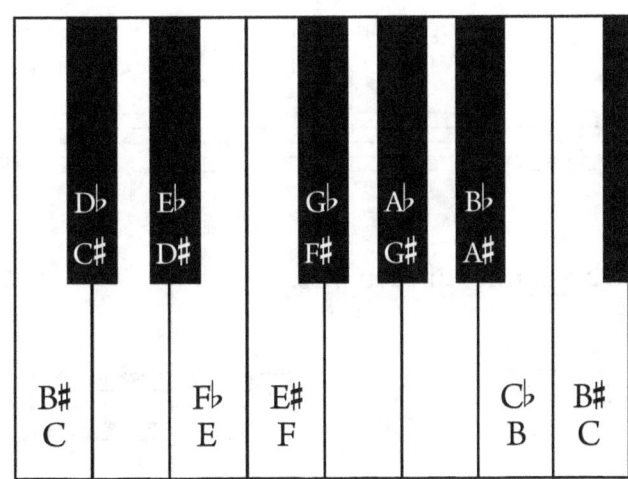

1. Give the enharmonic equivalents for the following notes.

F♯ _____   A♯ _____   F _____

B♭ _____   B _____   G♭ _____

C♯ _____   G♯ _____   D♭ _____

D♯ _____   C _____   A♭ _____

E♯ _____   B♭ _____   E♭ _____

Pitch and Notation

2
Time

Previous levels covered the time signatures 2/4, 3/4, and 4/4. Here, the bottom number tells us that the quarter note receives one beat and the top number tells us how many beats are in each measure. Time signatures with 2, 3, or 4 as the top number are in *simple time*.

Figure 2.1

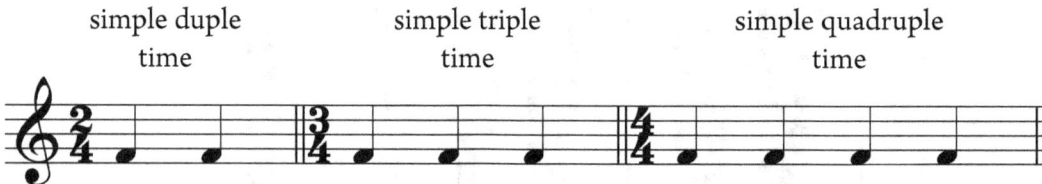

1. Add time signatures at the beginning of each line.

Simple Duple Time

In *simple duple time* the top number of the time signature is always 2. The time signature 2/4 is in simple duple time. Every measure is equal to 2 quarter notes.

Another simple duple time signature is 2/2. Here, the half note receives one beat and there are two beats in each measure. In other words, every measure is equal to two half notes. In all simple duple time signatures beat 1 is a *strong* beat and beat 2 is a *weak* beat. Study Figure 2.2.

2/2 two beats in each measure

the half note receives one beat

Figure 2.2

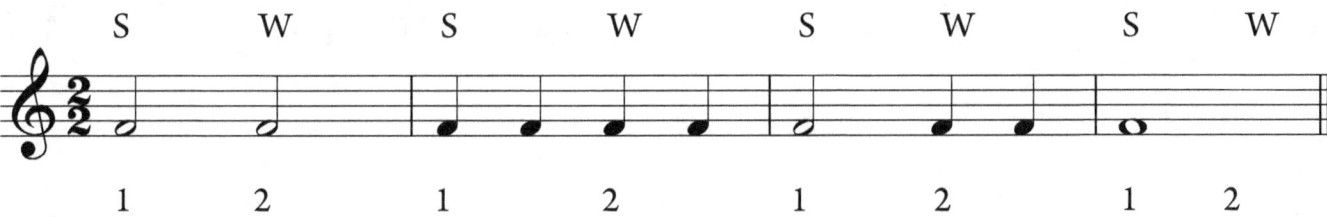

 This is an abbreviation for 2/2 time, sometimes called *cut time* or *alla breve*.

Figure 2.3 is in 2/8 time. Here, there are two beats in each measure and the eighth note receives one beat. Every measure is equal to 2 eighth notes. Beat 1 is strong and beat 2 is weak.

2/8 two beats in each measure

the eighth note receives one beat

Figure 2.3

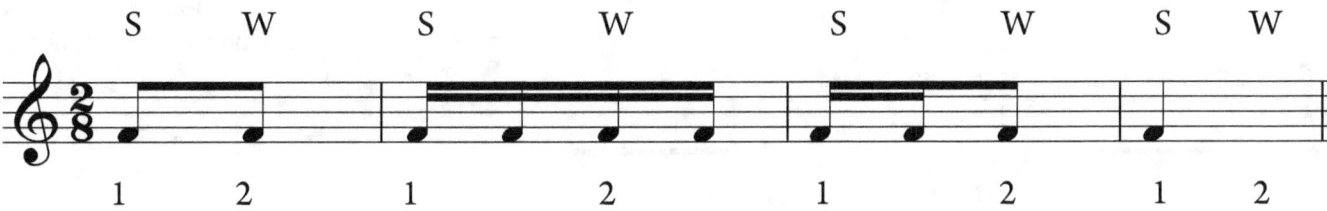

1. Using 2/4, 2/2 or 2/8 add the correct time signatures to the following melodies.

Simple Triple Time

In *simple triple time* the top number of the time signature is always 3. The time signature 3/4 is in simple triple time. Every measure is equal to 3 quarter notes.

Another simple triple time signature is 3/2. Here, the half note receives one beat and there are three beats in each measure. In other words, every measure is equal to three half notes. In all simple triple time signatures beat 1 is a *strong* beat and beats 2 and 3 are a *weak* beats. Study Figure 2.4.

3/2 three beats in each measure

the half note receives one beat

Figure 2.4

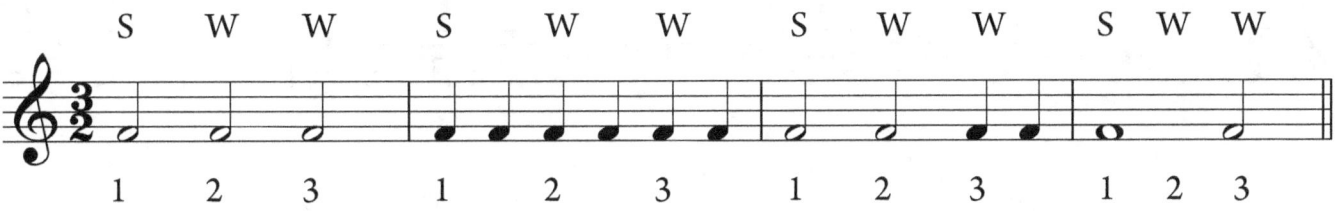

Figure 2.5 is in 3/8 time. Here, there are three beats in each measure and the eighth note receives one beat. Every measure is equal to 3 eighth notes. Beat 1 is strong and beats 2 and 3 are weak. *In 3/8 time all eighth and sixteenth notes are beamed into a complete bar.*

3/8 three beats in each measure

the eighth note receives one beat

Figure 2.5

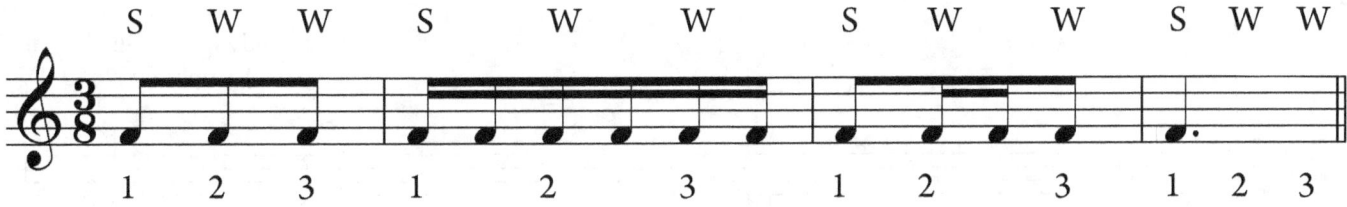

1. Add bar lines according to the time signatures.

Simple Quadruple Time

In *simple quadruple time* the top number of the time signature is always 4. The time signature 4/4 is in simple quadruple time. Every measure is equal to 4 quarter notes.

Another simple quadruple time signature is 4/2. Here, the half note receives one beat and there are four beats in each measure. In other words, every measure is equal to four half notes. In all simple quadruple time signatures beat 1 is a *strong* beat, 2 is a *weak* beat, 3 is a *medium* beat, and beat 4 is a *weak* beat. Study Figure 2.6.

4/2 four beats in each measure

the half note receives one beat

Figure 2.6

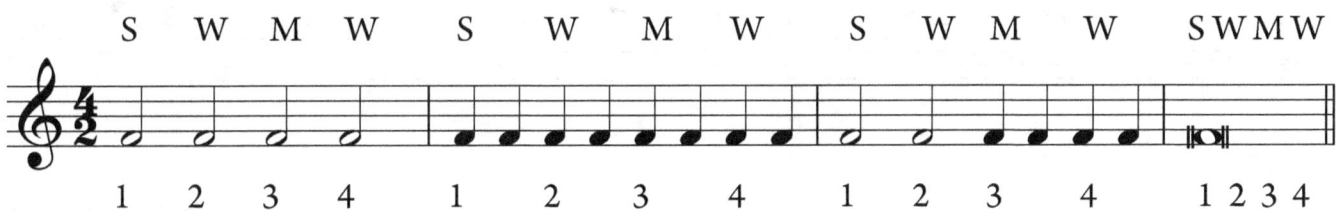

The **double whole note** and **double whole rest** equal 4 half notes. These are also called the **breve** and **breve rest**.

Note*** In 4/2 time a whole rest is not used for one complete measure of silence. Instead, the breve rest represents one complete measure of silence.

Figure 2.7 is in 4/8 time. Here, there are four beats in each measure and the eighth note receives one beat. Every measure is equal to 4 eighth notes.

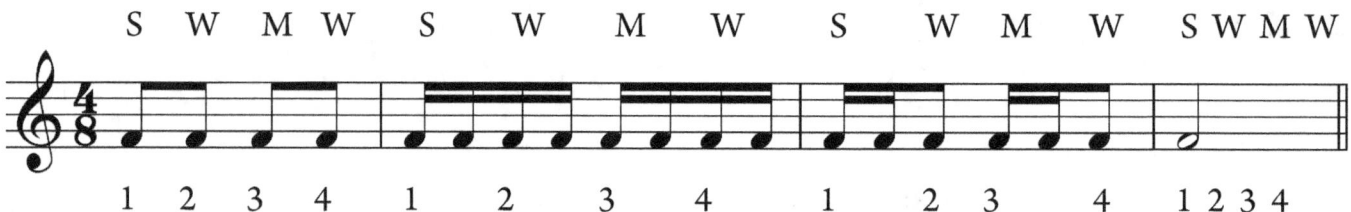

Figure 2.7

1. Add time signatures to the following melodies.

Girolamo Frescobaldi
Capriccio La Spagnoletta

Frederic Chopin
Nocturne Op. post.

Gustav Holst
Hymn Tune

Wolfgang Amadeus Mozart
Trio in C

2. Add bar lines according to the time signatures.

3. Add time signatures to the following lines.

The Dotted Whole Note and Rest

A dot after a note or rest increases its value by half. A dotted whole note is worth 1 whole note and 1 half note. This is the equivalent of a full measure in 3/2 time.

Figure 2.8

Rest Review

Figure 2.9 contains all the rests we have studied.
In 4/2 time a breve rest is used to represent one complete measure of silence.

Figure 2.9

1. Add one note to complete each measure according to the time signature.

2. Add one rest to complete each measure according to the time signature.

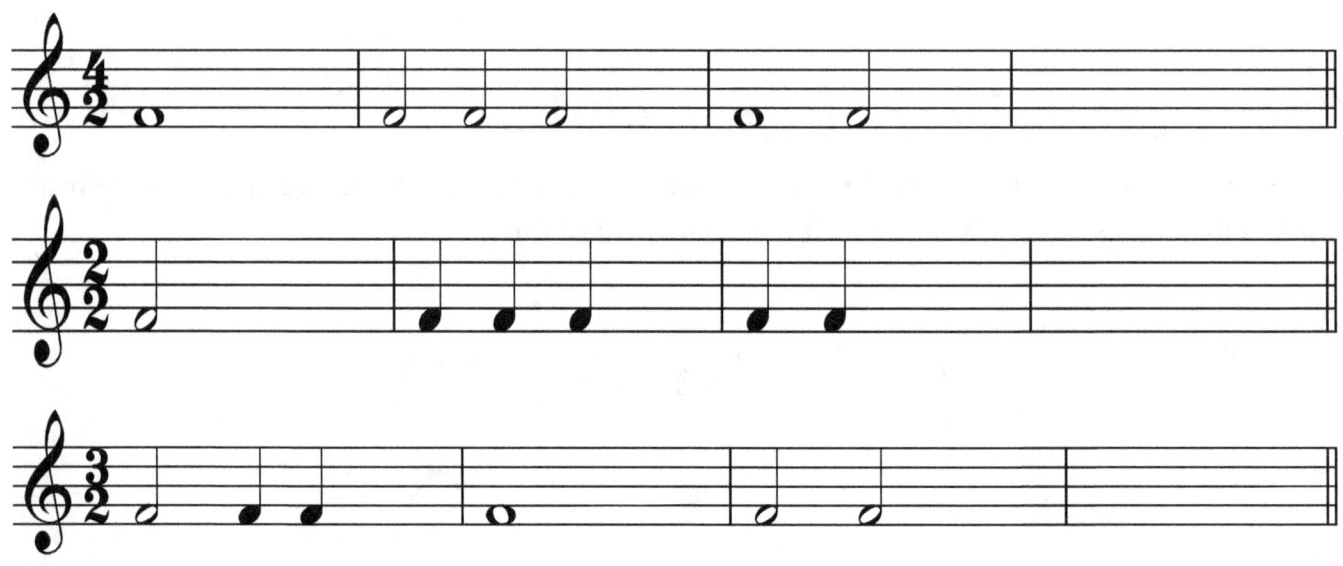

Triplet Review

When the beat is divided into three equal parts the result is a *triplet*. Triplets fall into a category of notes we call **tuplets**. A tuplet is a group of notes that do not follow the normal rules of counting.

An eighth note triplet consists of three notes played in the time of two eighth notes (1 quarter note). A sixteenth note triplet consists of 3 sixteenth notes played in the time of 2 sixteenth notes (1 eighth note). Figure 2.10 contains the triplets presented in previous levels.

Figure 2.10

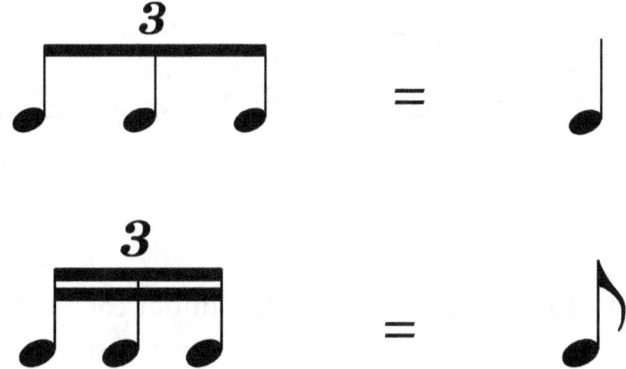

1. Add the correct time signature to each example.

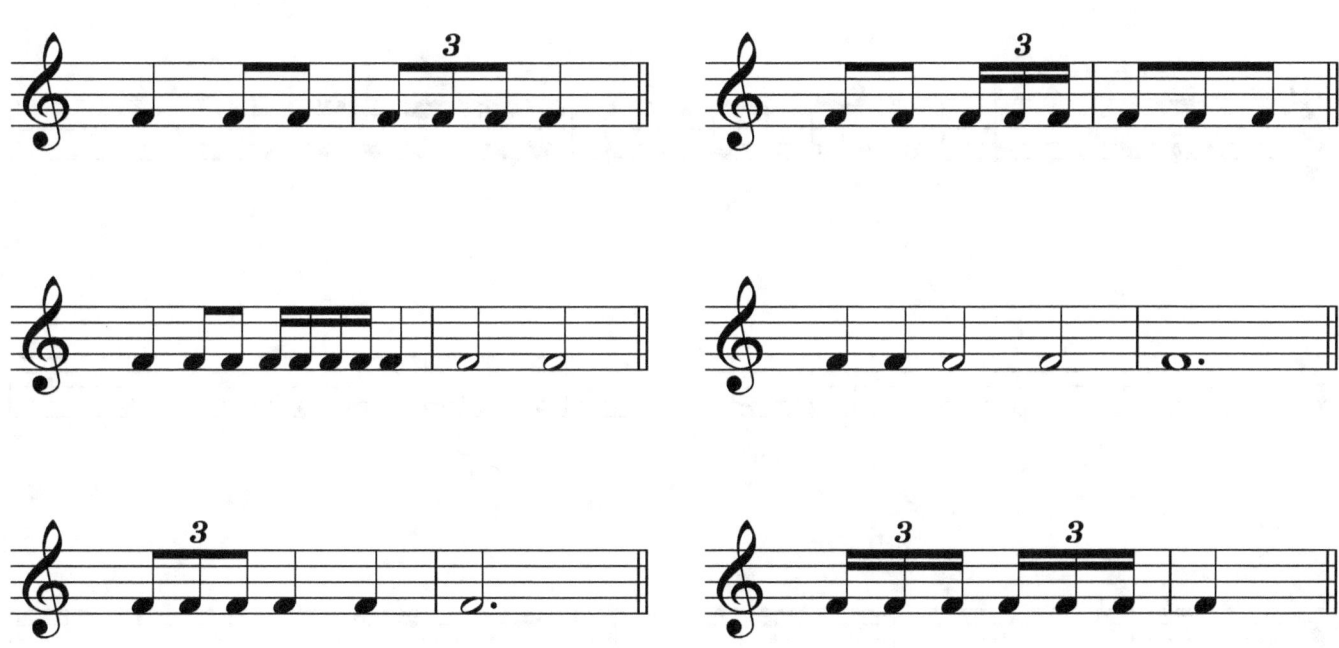

The Quarter Note Triplet

The quarter note triplet follows the triplet rule of three notes in the time of two. In this case one quarter note triplet equals two quarter notes or one half note. This triplet represents one beat in 2/2, 3/2, and 4/2 time.

Figure 2.11 shows quarter note triplets. Quarter note triplets do not have a beam like eighth note triplets. When there is no beam a bracket is added and the number is centered within the bracket. If the notes go up or down sometimes the bracket is angled to match the direction of the notes.

Figure 2.11

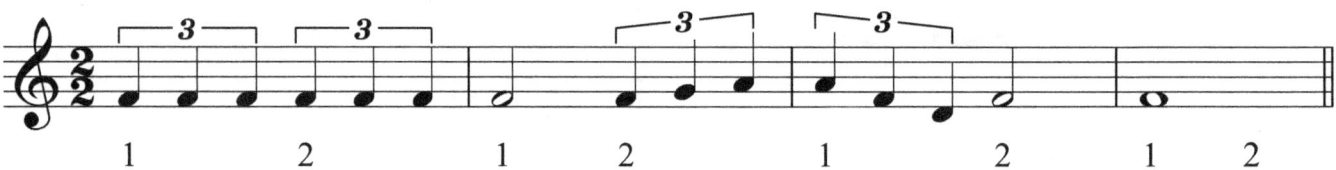

1. Add time signatures to the following lines. Write the beats under each measure.

Adding Rests in Simple Time

A whole rest represents a complete measure of silence in almost all time signatures. In 4/2 time a whole measure of silence is represented by a breve rest.

Figure 2.12

There are specific rules for adding rests to a measure in simple time. It is important to show each beat as clearly as possible. Each beat or each part of the beat must be completed before beginning the next beat.

In Figure 2.13 measure 2, each eighth note beat is completed with an eighth note rest. In measures 3 and 4, the sixteenth note has a sixteenth rest to complete part of the beat and then an eighth rest to complete the remainder of the beat.

Figure 2.13

In Figure 2.14 each beat is a half note. In measure 2, each quarter note beat is completed with a quarter note rest. You **cannot** join these two into one half rest. In measure 3, the sixteenth note has a sixteenth rest to complete the first part of the beat, an eighth rest to complete the next part and a quarter rest to complete the remainder of the beat. In m.4 the first beat needs a quarter rest to complete it. The second beat is completed from the back forward. The eighth note needs an eighth rest to complete a portion of the beat and a quarter rest to complete the rest of the beat.

Figure 2.14

In Figure 2.15, measure 3, the incomplete sixteenth note beats are completed separately with sixteenth note rests. This shows each beat. Joining these rests into one eighth rest is wrong.

Figure 2.15

1. Complete the following measures by adding the correct rest under each bracket.

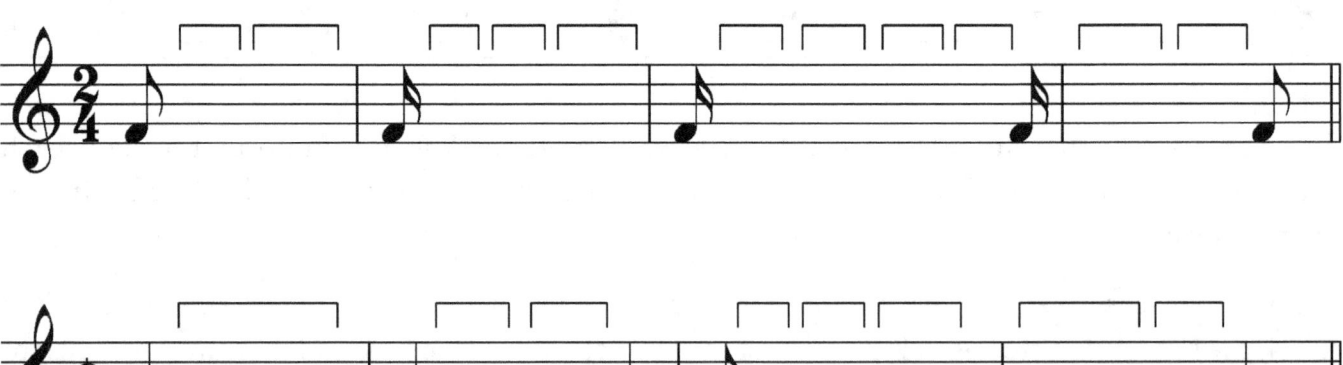

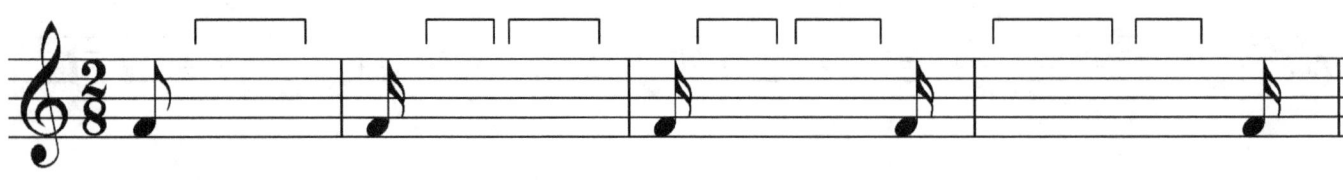

In simple triple time each beat or part of the beat should be completed first. Join beats 1 and 2, a strong and weak beat, into one rest. **Do not join beats 2 and 3, two weak beats, into one rest.** Never join two weak beats into one rest.

Figure 2.16

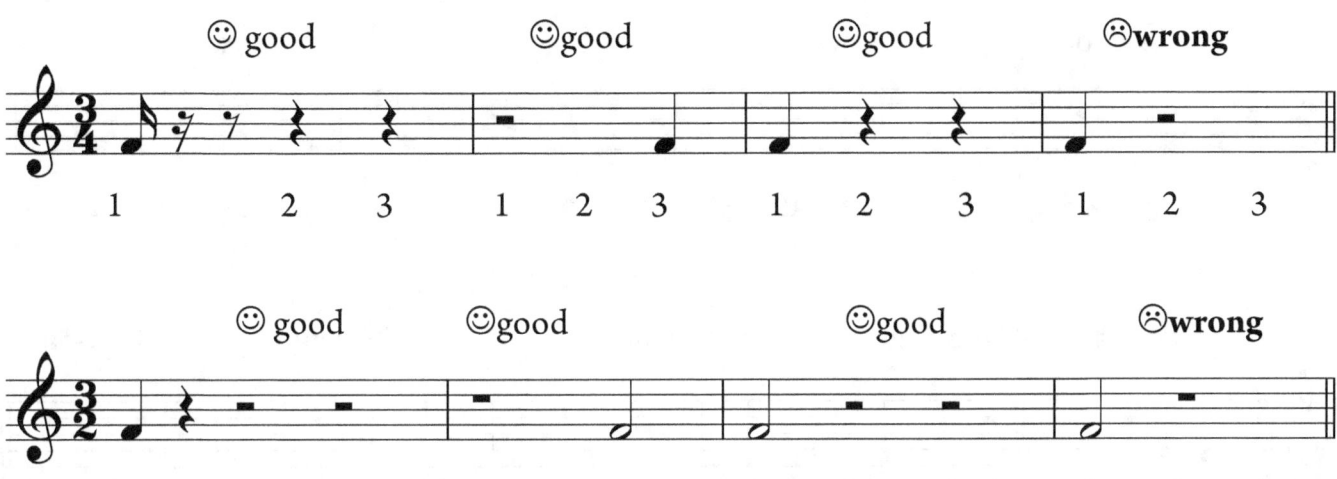

2. Complete the following measures by adding the correct rest under each bracket.

©San Marco Publications 2022

We never use rests larger than one beat unless it is in the first half or last half of a measure in simple quadruple time (4/4, 4/2, 4/8) or whole measure of silence. Join beats 1 and 2 and beats 3 and 4 into one rest. Never join beats 2 and 3, a weak beat and a medium beat, into one rest. As in all simple time signatures, finish any incomplete beats first. In 4/2 time a breve rest is used for a complete measure of silence.

Figure 2.17

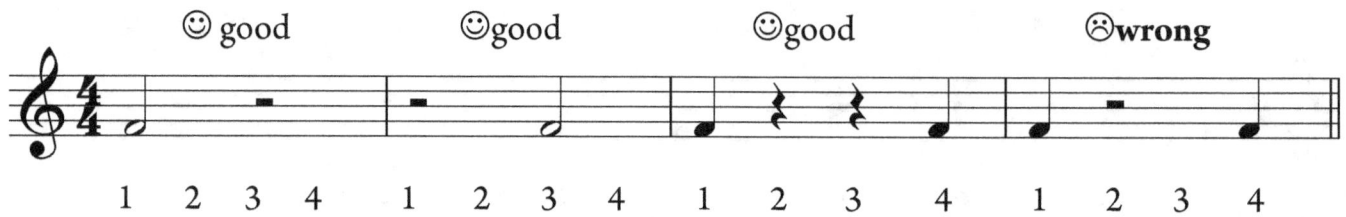

3. Complete the following measures by adding the correct rest under each bracket.

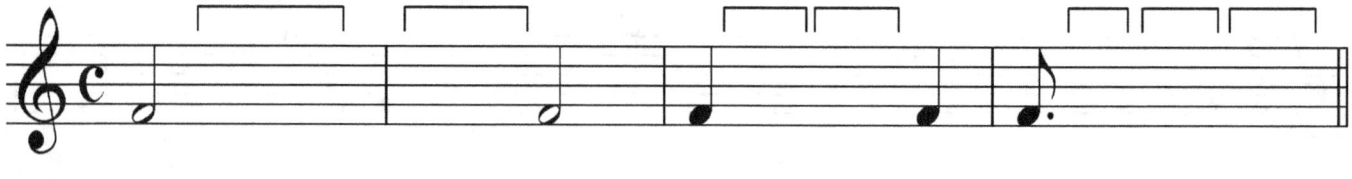

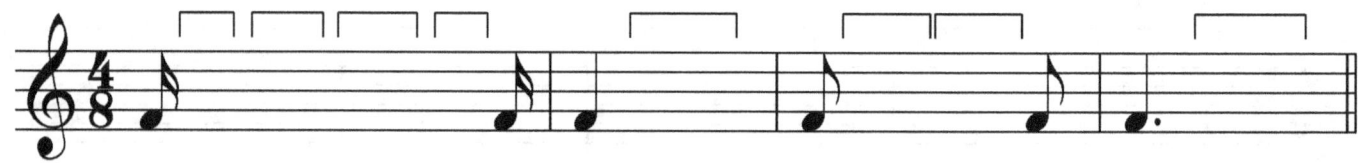

4. Add the correct rests under each bracket to complete the following measures.

Grouping Notes

In 2/2, 3/2 and 4/2 time.
Use a whole note instead of 2 tied half notes within a measure.

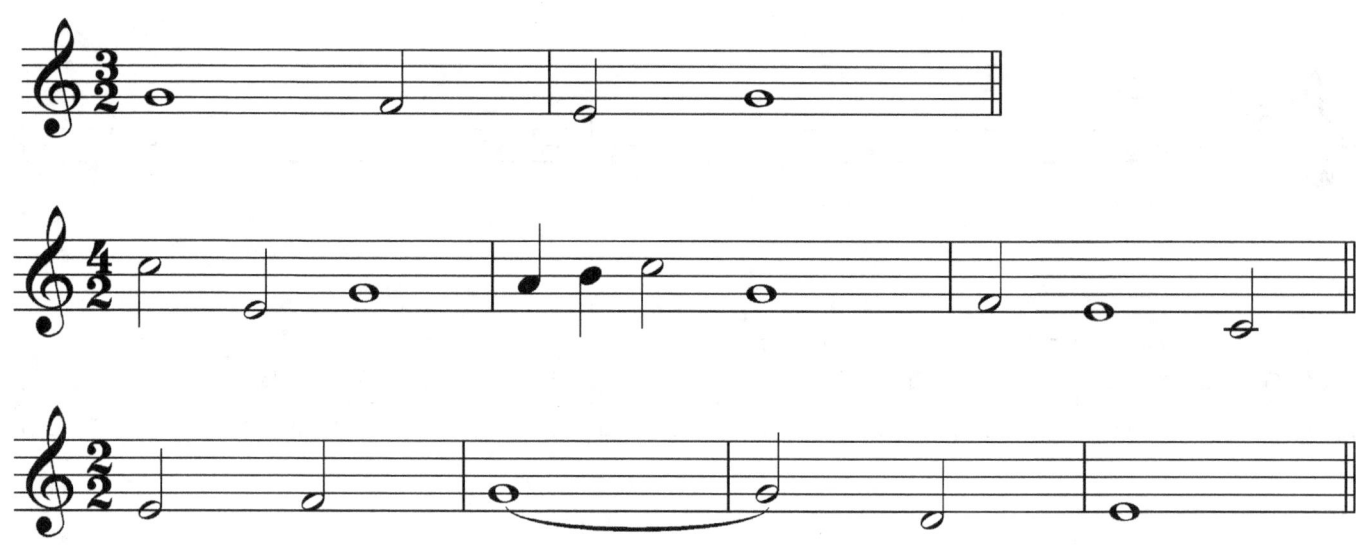

Beam eighth notes by half note beats.

Beam sixteenth notes by quarter note beats.

1. Rewrite the following rhythms grouping them correctly.

2. Rewrite the following melodies correcting any mistakes in the grouping of notes and rests. The first example is done for you.

Edvard Grieg
Norwegian Melody

Robert Schumann
Symphony No. 3

Gustav Mahler
Resurrection Symphony, I

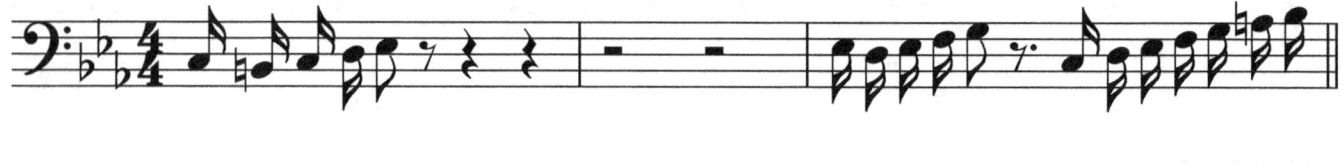

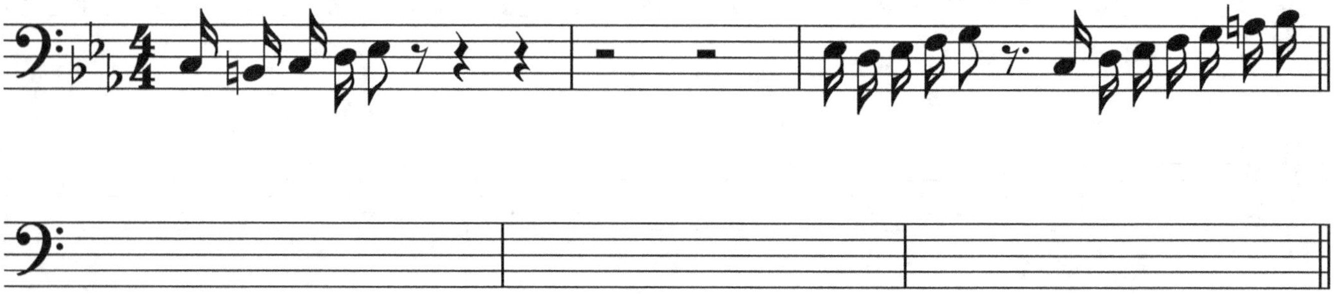

Compound Time

In simple time the beat can be divided into 2 equal parts. The top number of the time signature is 2, 3, or 4.

♩ = ♫ and 𝅗𝅥 = ♩ ♩

In simple time sometimes the beat can be divided into 3 equal parts using triplets.

♩ = ♪♪♪ (3) and 𝅗𝅥 = ♩♩♩ (3)

In *compound time* the top number of the time signature is 6, 9, or 12. The beat is divided into 3 parts. The main beat is a dotted note.

♩. = ♪♪♪

A New Time Signature

6/8 In this time signature, every measure adds up to 6 eighth notes.

In 6/8:

♪ = 1   ♩ = 2   ♩. = 3   𝅗𝅥. = 6

In 6/8 time we do not say there are 6 beats in each measure.
We say there are 2 beats in each measure and each measure contains 6 *pulses*.
Every beat is a group of 3 pulses. Since there are 2 beats, 3 + 3 = 6 pulses.
Therefore, 6/8 time is grouped into 2 groups of 3 pulses.
6/8 time is *compound duple time*. *Compound* refers to each beat grouped in 3 pulses, and *duple* refers to two beats in each measure.

Figure 2.18 shows the difference in the way beats are grouped in 3/4 and 6/8. Both time signatures are equal to 6 eighth notes, but 3/4 is grouped into 3 groups of 2 eighth notes and 6/8 into 2 groups of 3 eighth notes.

The accent structure for 6/8 time is: **Strong** weak weak   **Medium** weak weak

Figure 2.18

1. The following pieces are in 6/8 time. Circle the 2 main beats in each clef. Each beat consists of 3 pulses.

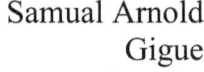

Samual Arnold
Gigue

Ludvig Schytte
Etude

2. Add time signatures to the following lines.

3. Rewrite the following rhythms grouping them according to the time signatures.

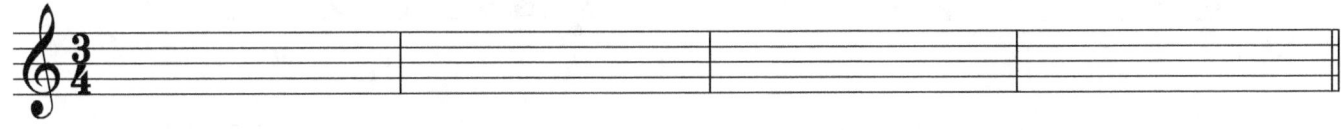

Rests in Compound Time

In compound time a whole rest is used to indicate one complete measure of silence. Figure 2.19 shows a complete measure of silence in 6/8 time.

Figure 2.19

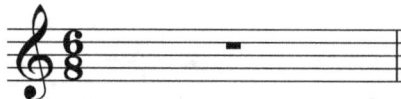

a. When adding rests to complete the first 2 pulses of a beat in 6/8 time, use one rest. In Figure 2.20**a** one quarter rest is used to complete the first 2 pulses of the beat.
b. When adding rests to complete the last 2 pulses of a beat in 6/8 time, use 2 rests. In Figure 2.20**b** 2 eighth rests are used to show pulses 2 and 3 of each beat.
c. Never join pulses 2 and 3 of a beat into one rest. This is wrong. Figure 2.20**c**.
d. In 6/8 time single beats are usually represented by one dotted quarter rest Figure 2.20**d**.
e. Although not that common, it is acceptable for a single beat to be written as a quarter rest followed by an eighth rest Figure 2.20**e**.

Figure 2.20

1. Add rests to complete each bar of 6/8 time.

©San Marco Publications 2022

2. Add rests under the brackets to complete each measure.

3

Major Scales

A major scale is a series of seven notes (eight with the repeated octave) that has a specific pattern of intervals. It starts and ends on the same note, the tonic. The tonic names the scale. If it starts and ends on D, the tonic is D, and it is the D major scale. Let's review the order of intervals in the major scale. Major scales are built on the following pattern of whole steps and half steps:

whole step - whole step - half step - whole step - whole step - whole step - half step

The scale can also be divided into two four note sections called tetrachords as shown in Figure 3.1. Each tetrachord is WWH with a W between the two (WWH W WWH).

Scale tones can be labeled with a number and a small sign called a *caret* on top ($\hat{1}, \hat{2}$, etc.). This indicates a ***scale degree***. The first note of a scale is scale degree one ($\hat{1}$), The second is scale degree two ($\hat{2}$), etc.

Figure 3.1

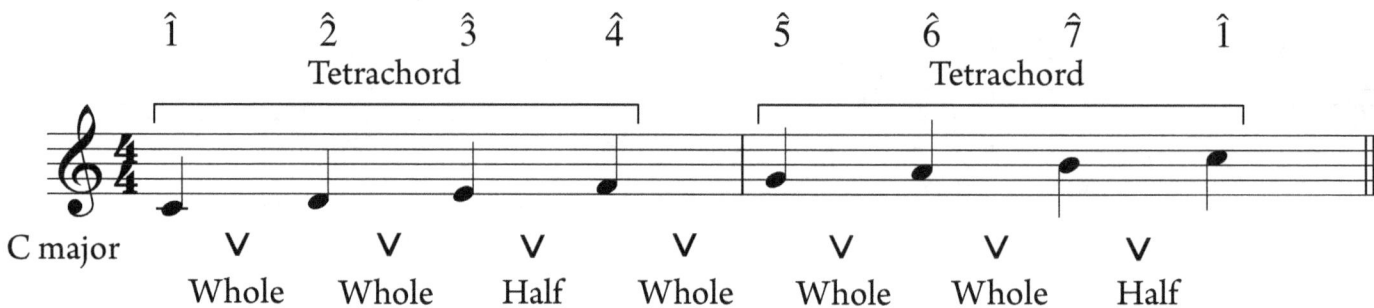

The Keys of E major and A flat Major

At this level we will learn two new major scales. E major has four sharps and A♭ major has four flats. These scales follow the same pattern of whole steps and half steps as all major scales.

Figure 3.2 contains the scales of E major and A♭ major.

Figure 3.2

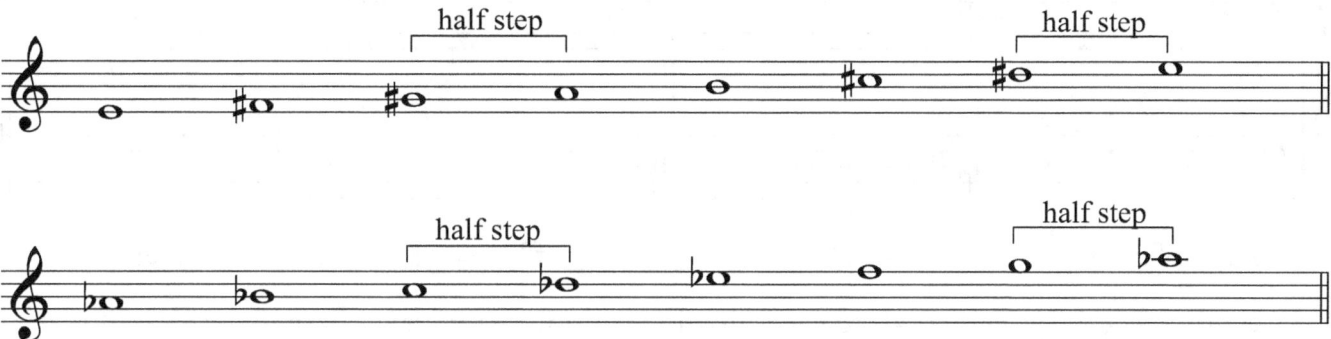

Key Signature Review

The first level of organization that a piece of music receives is the key. Music that uses a key signature is considered **tonal music**.

Each key signature is also the name of the major scale with the same name. For example, the key of A major will give you the correct accidentals for the scale of A major. This music is **diatonic**. This is music that is centered around a single tone or the **tonic**. A piece in A major is a tonal piece centered around the note A, the tonic.

Sharps and flats are placed in a specific order in a key signature. This is the order of the first four sharps as they appear in a key signature: **F C G D**.

Figure 3.3 contains the key signatures up to four sharps on the grand staff.

Figure 3.3

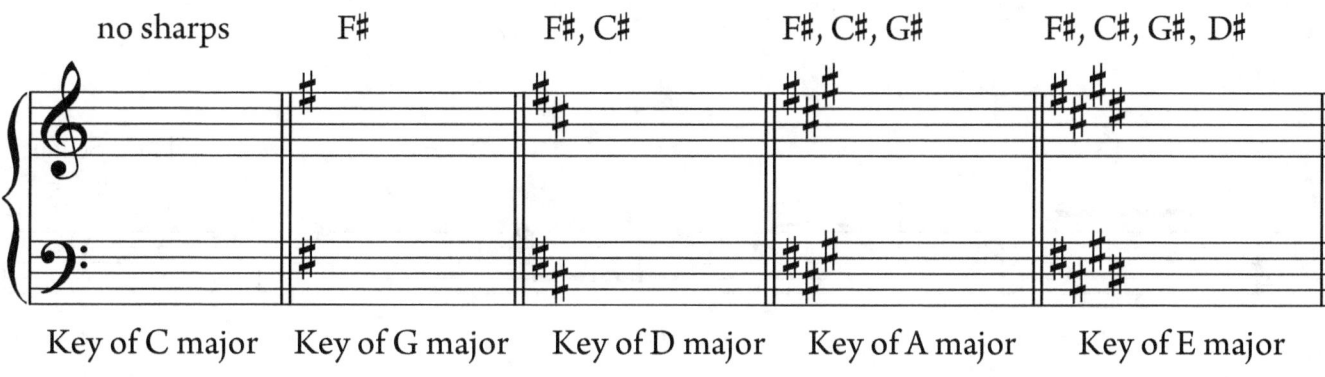

This is the order of the first four flats as they appear in a key signature: **B E A D**.

Figure 3.4 contains the key signatures up to four flats on the grand staff.

Figure 3.4

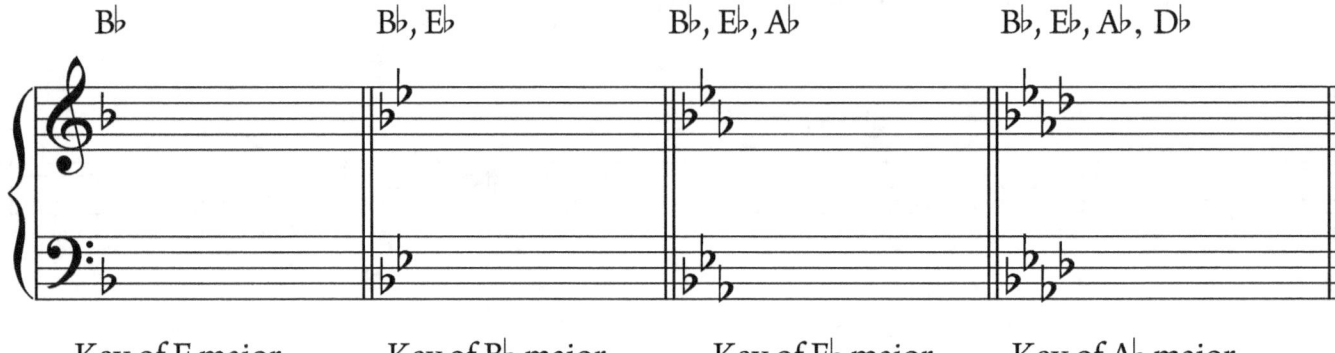

1. Insert the necessary accidentals to the following melodies. The key is named for each.

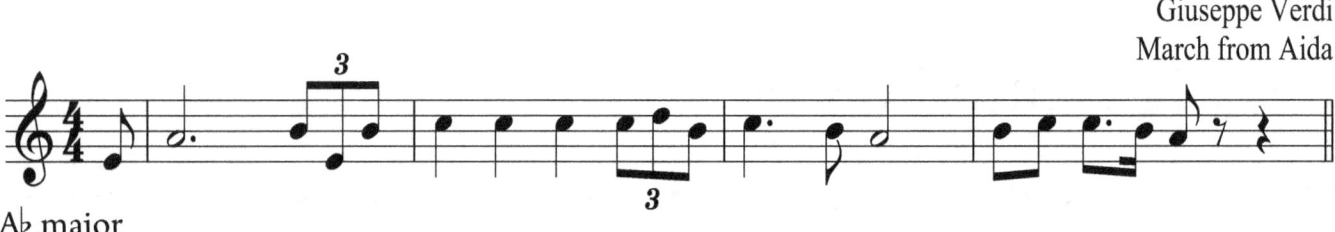

A♭ major

E major

D major

A major

2. Write the following key signatures on the grand staff.

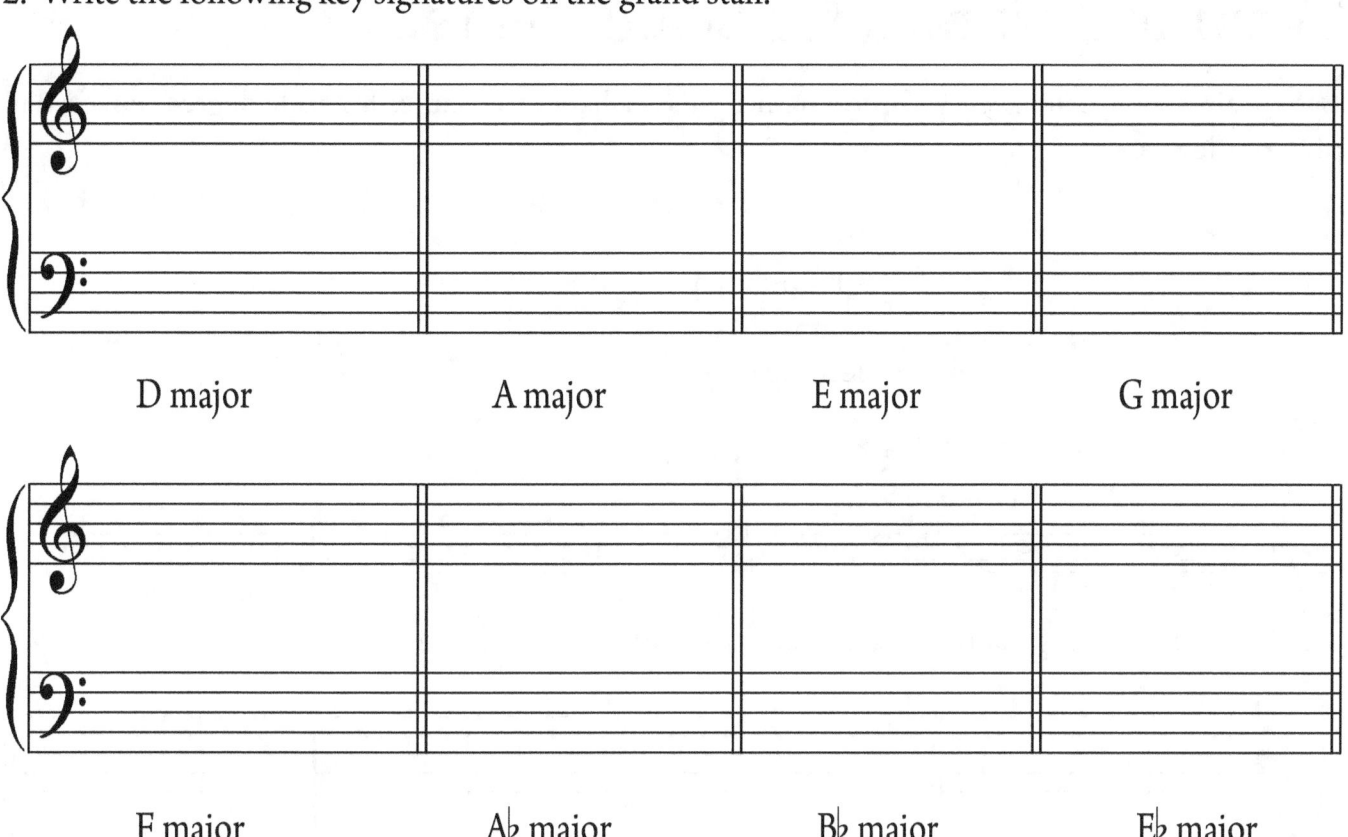

D major   A major   E major   G major

F major   A♭ major   B♭ major   E♭ major

These are the major key signatures covered in this level.

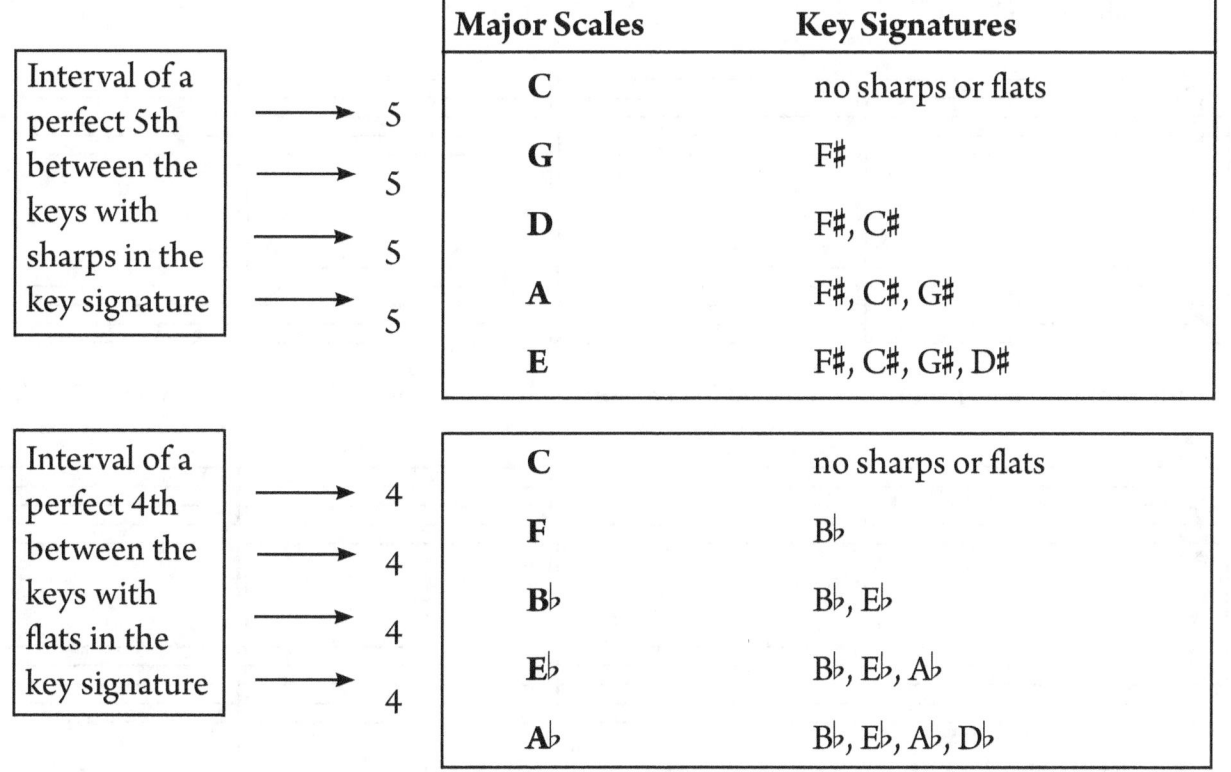

©San Marco Publications 2022

Technical Names for Scale Degrees

Each scale degree can have a technical name. This is a list of the names for scale degrees covered in previous levels.

$\hat{1}$	tonic
$\hat{4}$	subdominant
$\hat{5}$	dominant
$\hat{7}$	leading tone

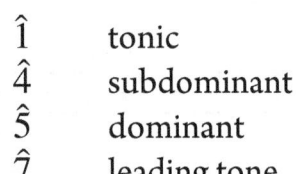

Figure 3.5

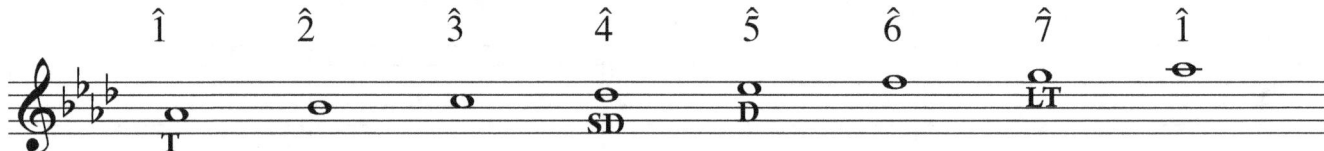

1. Write the following major key signatures and notes on the grand staves.

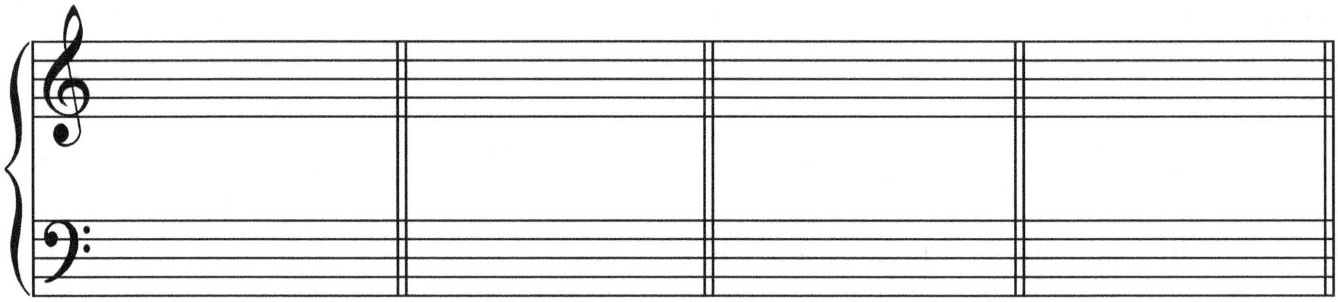

dominant in D major | tonic in E major | leading tone in B♭ major | tonic in E♭ major

subdominant in A♭ major | dominant in G major | subdominant in E♭ major | tonic in F major

leading tone in C major | tonic in G major | dominant in E♭ major | dominant in A major

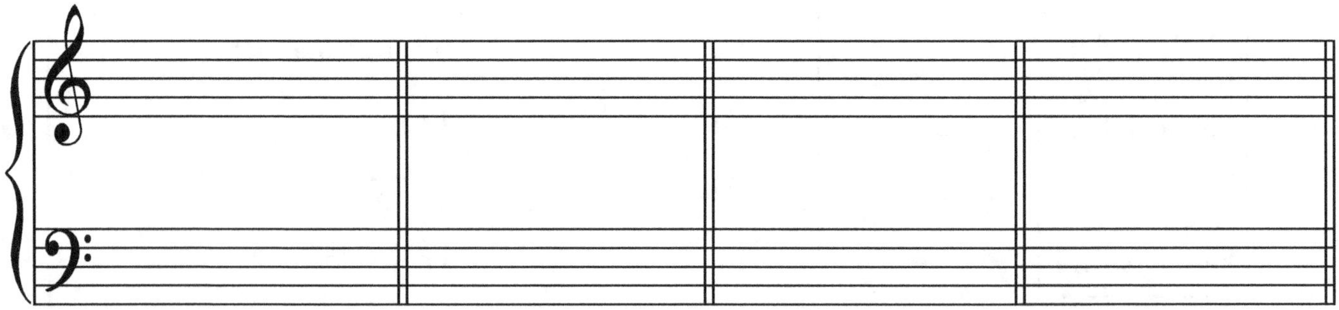

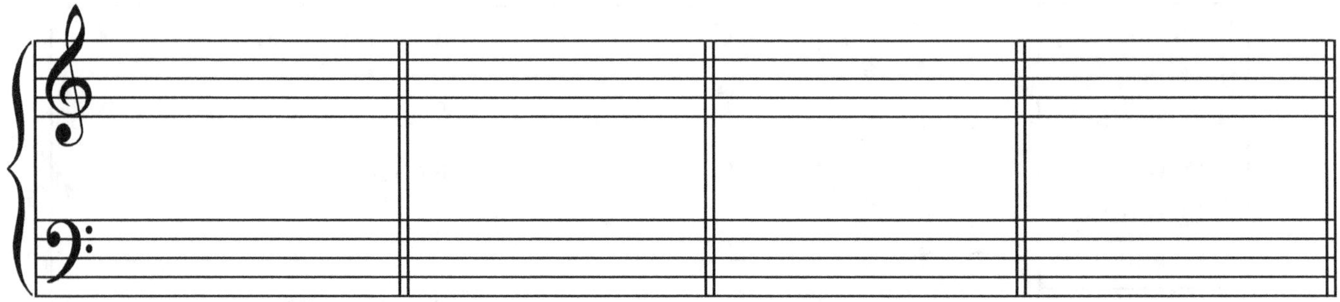

2. Write the following scales ascending and descending in wholes notes using a key signature for each.

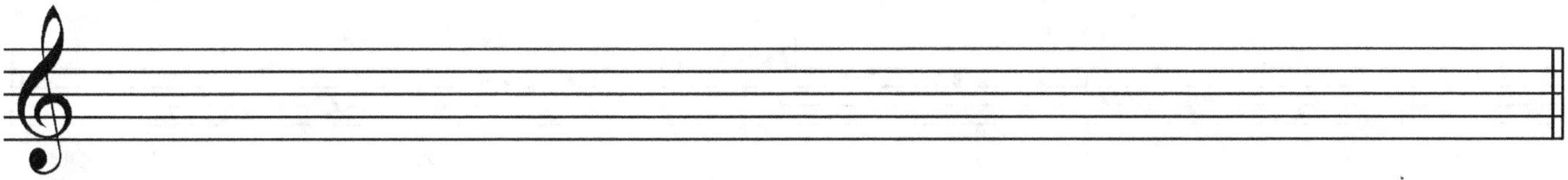

E major

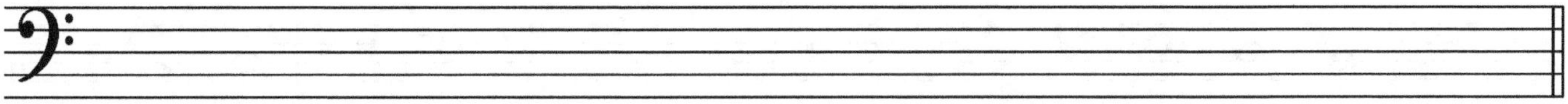

A♭ major

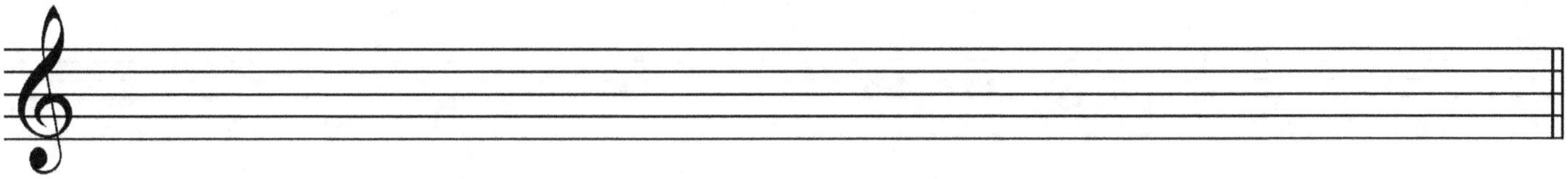

B♭ major

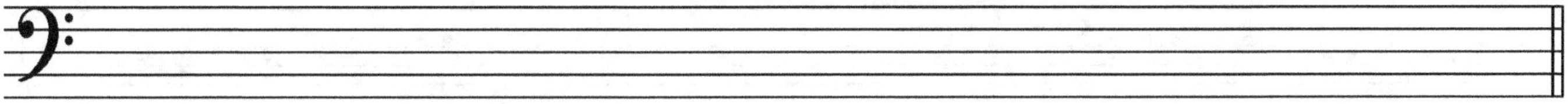

G major

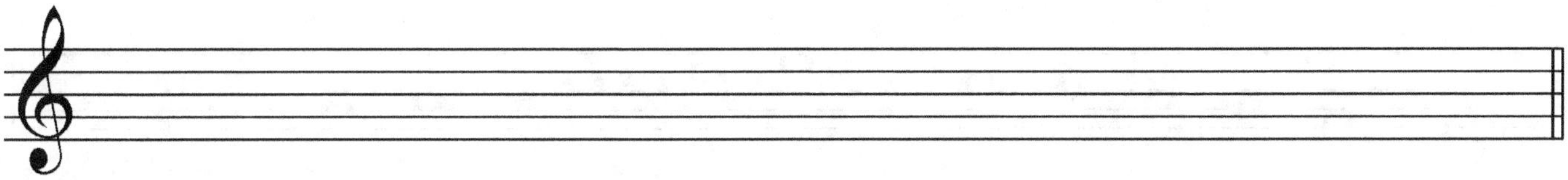

A major

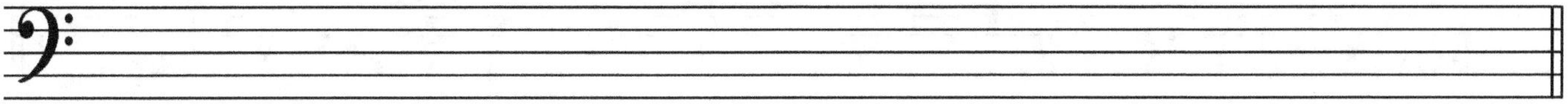

F major

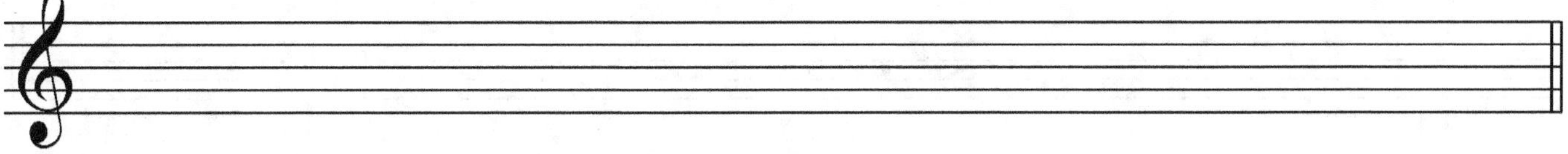

E♭ major

Major Scales

3. Add clefs and accidentals to create the following major scales.

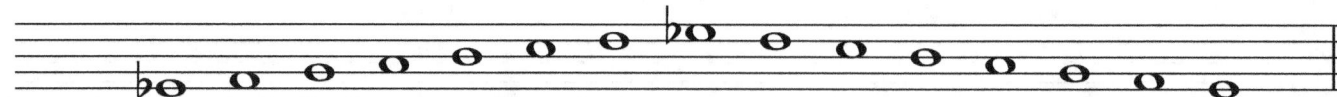

E♭ major

A major

E major

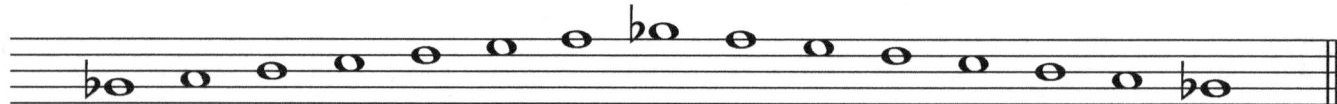

B♭ major

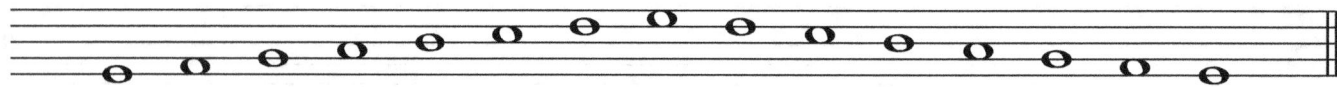

G major

A♭ major

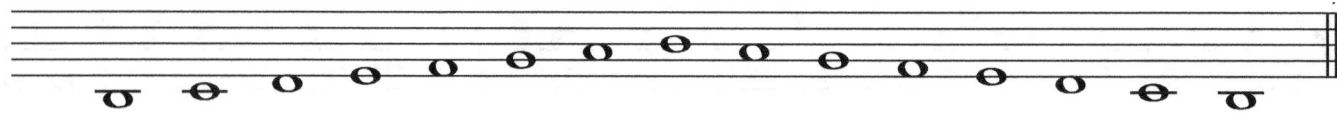

D major

4. Write the following scales using key signatures ascending and descending in half notes.

The major scale with 4 flats

The major scale with D as the leading tone

The major scale with E as the dominant

The major scale with B♭ as the subdominant

The major scale with two sharps

The major scale with A as the subdominant

The major scale with F as the dominant

4
History 1

George Frideric Handel (1685 - 1759) Baroque Era

George Frideric Handel was born on February 23, 1685, in Halle Germany. His father, a barber-surgeon, wanted his son to be a lawyer. However, Handel loved music and practiced on a small keyboard instrument called a clavichord, given to him by his aunt.

In 1693, while visiting the royal court, Handel had an opportunity to play the great organ. When the Duke heard him play, he convinced his father to give him musical training. Handel studied with the organist of St. Michel's in Halle. He learned how to compose, and how to play violin and oboe as well as organ and harpsichord.

In 1702, Handel followed his father's suggestion and entered law school at the University of Halle. After his father's death in the following year, he left his law studies and accepted a position as the organist at Halle Cathedral. The following year, he moved to Hamburg and worked as a violinist and harpsichordist at the opera house. It was there that Handel's first operas were written and produced.

In 1710, Handel accepted the position of Kapellmeister to George, Elector of Hanover, who was soon to be King George I of Great Britain. In 1712, he settled in England where George's wife Queen Anne gave him a yearly income.

Handel wrote operas and oratorios plus music for instruments and ensembles. In 1727, he applied for British citizenship and adopted England as his new home. When King George I died, Handel wrote the music for the coronation of the new king. *Zadok the Priest*, one of these compositions, is still performed today at British coronations.

By 1741, Handel had completed the oratorio Messiah. The first performance of Messiah was given in Ireland in 1742 and was a great success. Many people, to this day, stand during the performance of the "Hallelujah Chorus." Some historians disagree, but the legend is that when the king first heard the "Hallelujah Chorus" he rose to his feet, overcome with emotion. Since the king stood, so did the entire audience. The tradition continues to this day of standing when the "Hallelujah Chorus" from Messiah is performed.

Handel died on April 14, 1759. He was given the honor of a state funeral and was buried in Westminster Abby in London, England. More than 3,000 people attended his funeral.

What is an Oratorio?

An *oratorio* is a large composition for orchestra, choir, and soloists based on a religious theme. Some of the components of an oratorio are:

- *overture* - the musical introduction to the oratorio.
- *recitative* - a kind of musical declamation used during the oratorio, sung in the rhythm of ordinary speech often with many words on the same note.
- *aria* - an accompanied song for a solo voice.
- *chorus* - a large group of singers that performs together with an orchestra.

Messiah

Messiah is an oratorio composed in 1741 by George Frideric Handel. The *libretto*, which is the term used for the text of the oratorio, is based on verses from the Old and New Testaments of the Bible.

It is believed that Handel composed Messiah in only three or four weeks in August and September of 1741. What makes this amazing is the scale of this work. The score is 259 pages, and it takes nearly two hours to perform.

The "Hallelujah Chorus" from Messiah

The "Hallelujah Chorus" is part of Handel's Messiah. It is written for a chorus consisting of soprano, alto, tenor and bass with orchestra. The voices in a four part chorus are:

- *soprano* - sung by womens high voices
- *alto* - sung by womens low voices
- *tenor* - sung by mens high voices
- *bass* - sung by mens low voices

The text for "Hallelujah Chorus" comes from the book of Revelation in the New Testament. The word 'Hallelujah" means praise the Lord and is used in worship as an expression of rejoicing.
Text:
>Hallelujah!
>For the Lord God omnipotent reigneth;
>The kingdom of this world is become the kingdom of our Lord and of his Christ;
>and He shall reign for ever and ever.
>King of Kings and Lord of Lords.
>Hallelujah!

Figure 4.1 contains the opening of the chorus from the Hallelujah Chorus. Each voice part of the chorus receives its own staff line.

Hallelujah Chorus uses a technique called **word painting**. Word painting, sometimes called tone painting or text painting, is the technique of writing music that mirrors the actual meaning of a song.

In Hallelujah chorus low notes symbolize the world while the kingdom of the Lord is sung on high notes. The Hallelujah section has a joyful sound characterized by arpeggios and chromatic notes occurring in a major scale. The line *"for ever and ever"* is repeated over and over.

Figure 4.1

Review 1

1. Rewrite the following melodies in the other clef without changing the pitch.

Wolfgang Amadeus Mozart
Piano Concerto K270

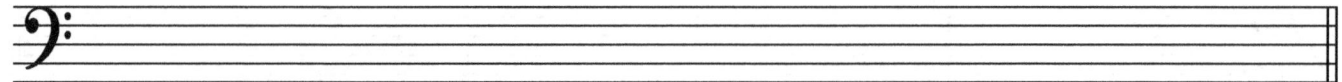

Mikhail Glinka
Souvenir of a Night in Madrid

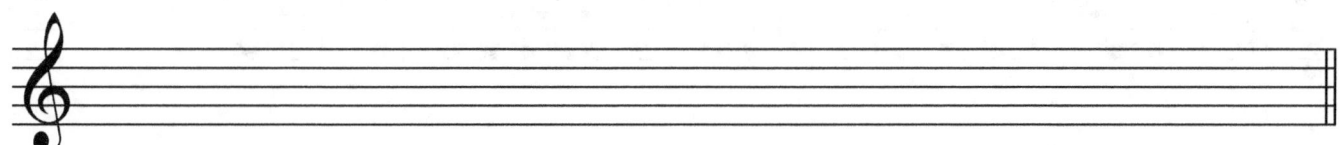

2. Give the enharmonic equivalents for the following notes.

C# _____   G# _____   F _____

A♭ _____   B _____   G♭ _____

F# _____   A# _____   E♭ _____

D# _____   C _____   B♭ _____

3. Add the correct rests under each bracket to complete the following measures.

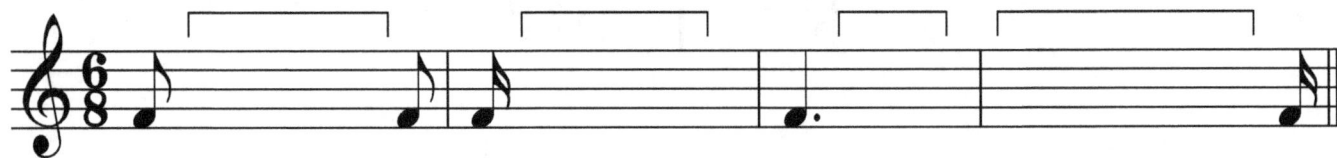

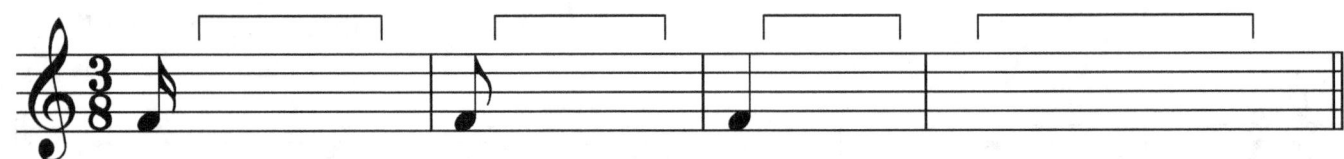

4. Add bar lines according to the time signatures.

5. Write the following scales ascending and descending. Label the leading tone in each.

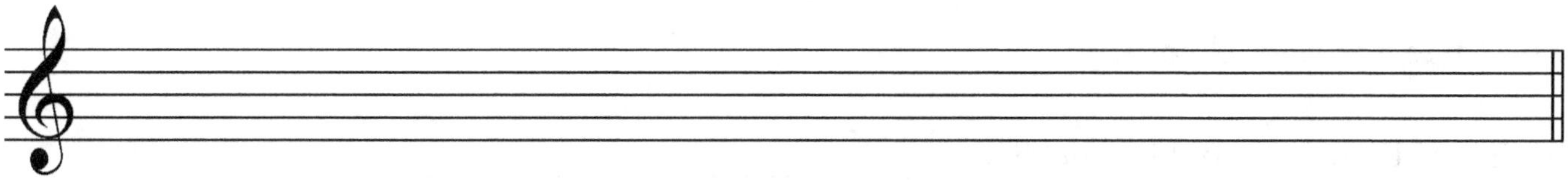

D major

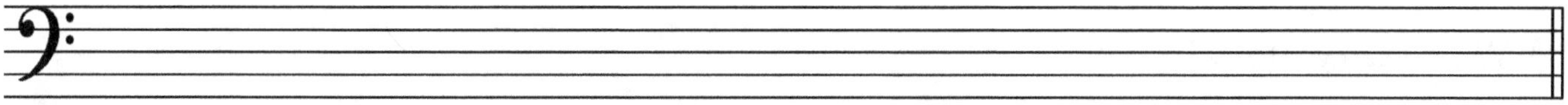

E♭ major

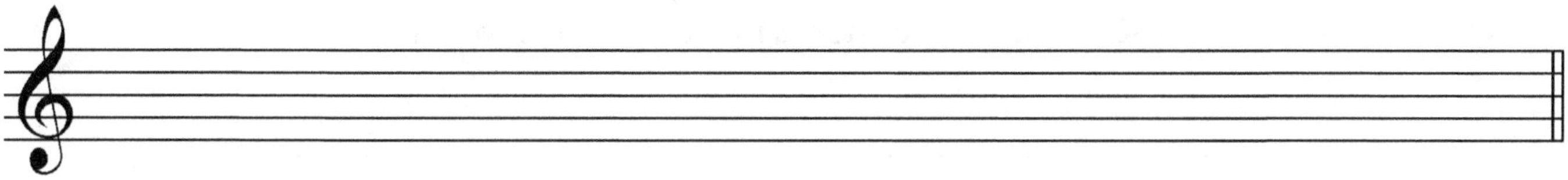

G major

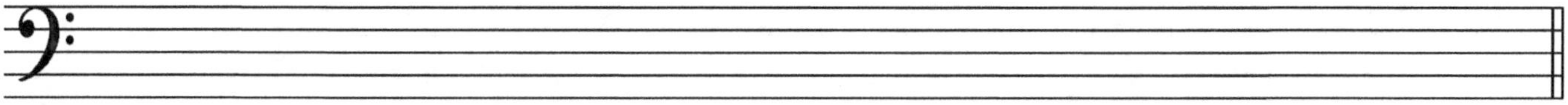

B♭ major

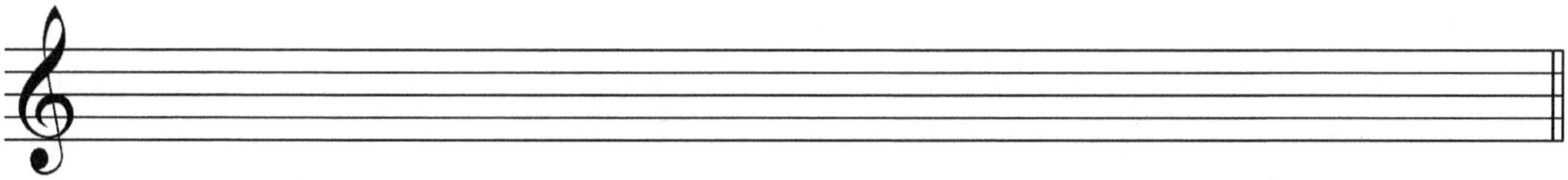

E major

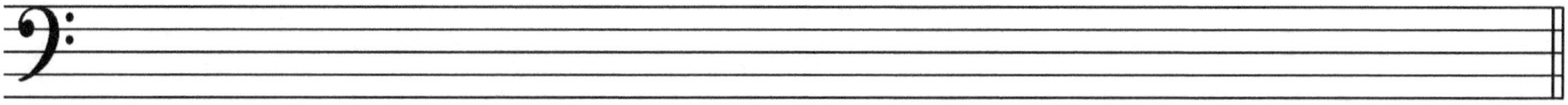

A♭ major

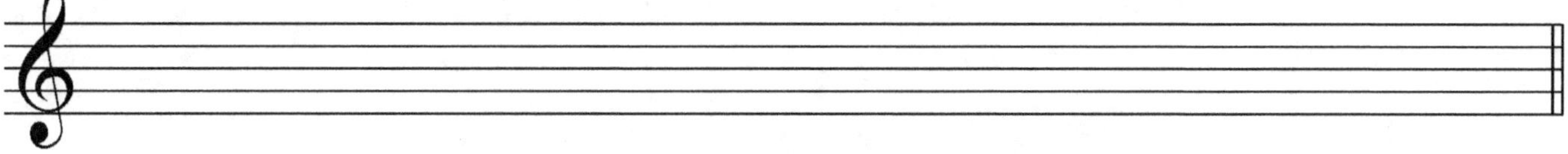

F major

Review 1

6. Answer the following questions.

a) Where was Handel born? _____

b) In what music era did Handel live? _____

c) What country did Handel adopt as his new home? _____

d) What is an oratorio? _____

e) When did Handel compose Messiah? _____

f) What voices make up the 4 parts of the chorus in Hallelujah Chorus?

   _____ _____ _____ _____

g) What is word painting? _____

_____

h) Give one example of word painting in Hallelujah Chorus. _____

_____

5
Minor Scales

Relative Keys

Every major key has a *relative minor*. They share the same key signature and are called *relative keys*. The relationship between these relative keys is shown in Figure 5.1. The tonic of the relative minor is located on scale degree $\hat{6}$ of the major scale. Scale degree $\hat{6}$ in C major is A. A minor is the relative minor of C major. They each have the same key signature, no sharps or flats.

Figure 5.1

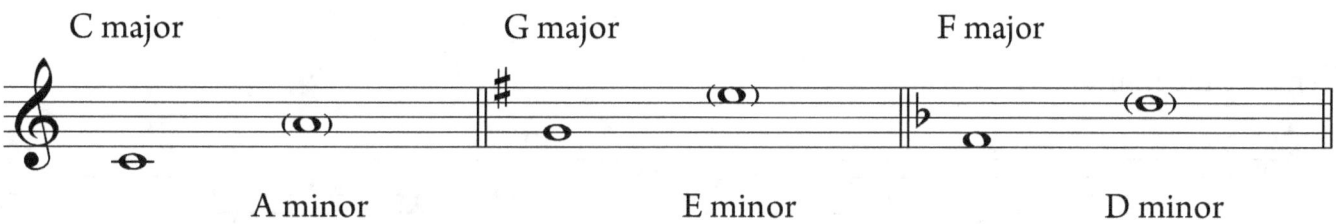

1. For the following examples: Name the major key. Write the tonic of the relative minor with a note in brackets. Name the relative minor key.

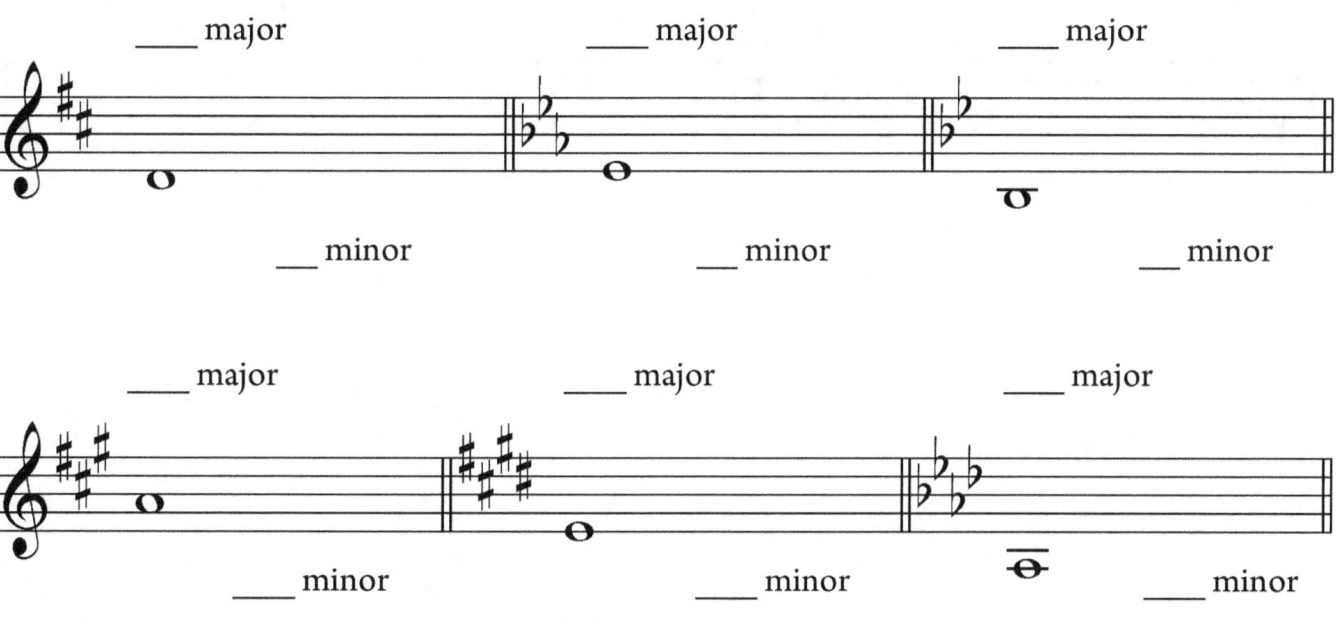

Minor Scale Review

There are three types of minor scales:

1. **natural minor**: uses the same key signature as its relative major.
2. **harmonic minor**: is the natural minor with $\hat{7}$ raised one half step.
3. **melodic minor**: is the natural minor with $\hat{6}$ and $\hat{7}$ raised one half step ascending, and lowered one half step descending.

Figure 5.2 shows all three versions of the D minor scale.

Figure 5.2

D natural minor

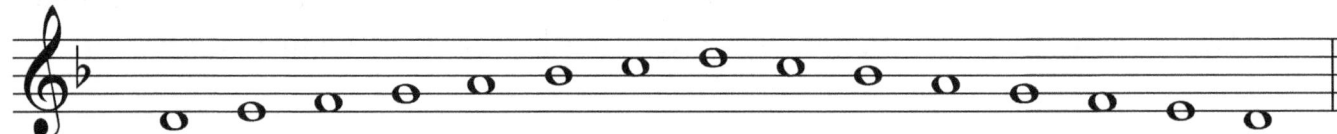

D harmonic minor

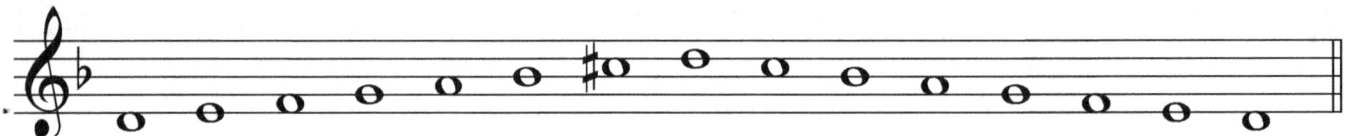

D melodic minor

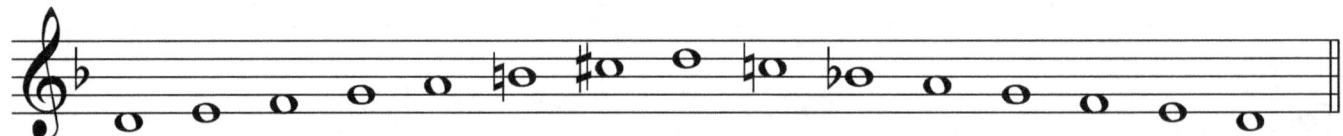

The table in Figure 5.3 shows the minor scales that are required for this level.

Figure 5.3

Minor Key	Key Signature	Harmonic form	Melodic form	
		Raise $\hat{7}$ in ascending and descending scales	Ascending raise $\hat{6}$ and $\hat{7}$	Descending lower $\hat{7}$ and $\hat{6}$
A	no sharps or flats	G♯	F♯, G♯	G♮, F♮
E	F♯	D♯	C♯, D♯	D♮, C♮
B	F♯, C♯	A♯	G♯, A♯	A♮, G♮
F♯	F♯, C♯, G♯	E♯	D♯, E♯	E♮, D♮
C♯	F♯, C♯, G♯, D♯	B♯	A♯, B♯	B♮, A♮
D	B♭	C♯	B♮, C♯	C♮, B♭
G	B♭, E♭	F♯	E♮, F♯	F♮, E♭
C	B♭, E♭, A♭	B♮	A♮, B♮	B♭, A♭
F	B♭, E♭, A♭, D♭	E♮	D♮, E♮	E♭, D♭

The Leading Tone and the Subtonic

There are two technical names for $\hat{7}$ in minor keys. When $\hat{7}$ is raised and is a half step from the tonic, it is called the **leading tone**. In the natural minor and the descending melodic minor where $\hat{7}$ is not raised and is a whole step away from the tonic, it is called the **subtonic**. When it is a whole step away, it does not sound like it is leading to the tonic. That's why it is called the subtonic.

Figure 5.4 shows the A melodic minor scale. The leading tone (G♯) occurs in the ascending portion, and the subtonic (G♮) occurs in the descending portion.

Figure 5.4

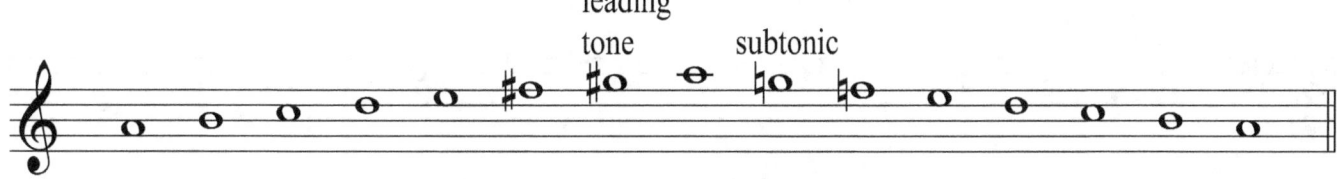

1. Name the key and following scales as natural, harmonic or melodic. e.g. *D harmonic minor*.

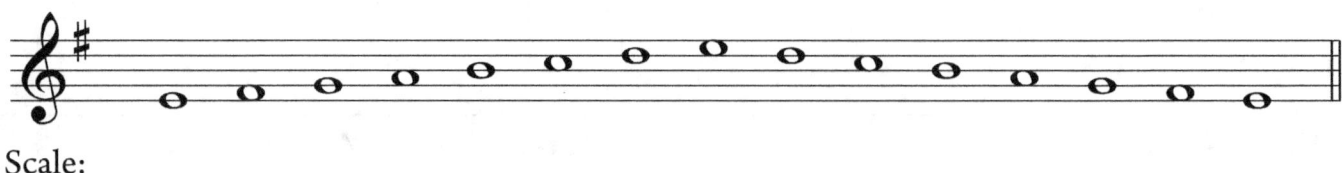

Scale:_____

Scale:_____

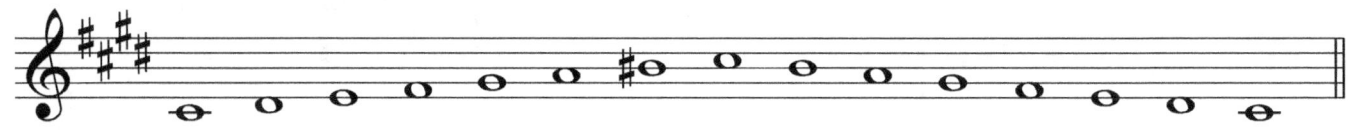

Scale:_____

Scale:_____

Scale:_____

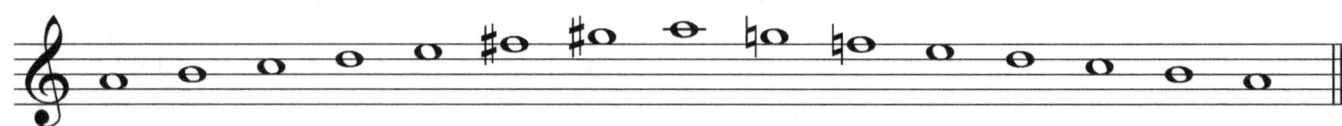

Scale:_____

Scale:_____

©San Marco Publications 2022   Minor Scales

2. Write the following scales ascending and descending in quarter notes using a key signature. Label the leading tones (LT).

C# harmonic minor

F melodic minor

D natural minor

F# harmonic minor

C melodic minor

B natural minor

E harmonic minor

3. Write the following scales ascending and descending in half notes using a key signature. Label the subtonic notes (ST).

The harmonic minor scale with the key signature of 4 flats

The melodic minor scale with the key signature of 2 sharps

The natural minor scale with G as the subtonic

The harmonic minor scale with F♯ as the leading tone

The melodic minor scale with C♯ as the tonic

The natural minor with G as the dominant

The harmonic minor scale with A major as its relative major

Parallel Keys and Scales

The scales covered to this point may also be known as **modes**. Mode is just another name for the word scale.

Thus far you have learned about the major mode and the three minor modes – natural, harmonic and melodic. Composers often move back and forth between the major and minor modes within the same piece to make their compositions interesting.

Because of the common notes and key signatures, composers may also change keys, or modulate back and forth between relative major and minor keys. For example, a piece in G minor often moves to the key of B♭ major. G minor and B♭ major are relative minor and major keys and share the same key signature of B♭ and E♭. Because of this, many notes are the same between the two keys, and it is easy to move between them.

Composers may also keep the tonic the same but change the mode of the piece from major to minor, or vice-versa. For example a piece in C major might change keys to C minor. These two keys are related because they share the same tonic, C.

Major and minor keys that use the same tonic are known as **parallel** major and minor keys. For example, F major and F minor are parallel keys. They both have F as the tonic.

1. Write the following scales ascending and descending in whole notes using a key signature. Name each scale.

G major

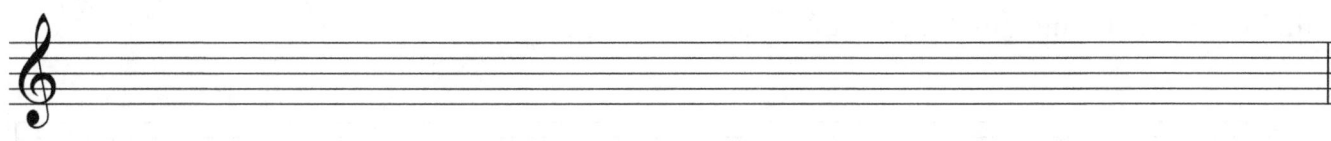

G major's parallel minor, harmonic form

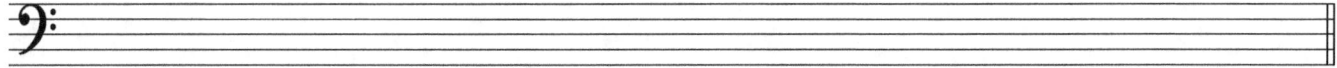

G major's relative minor, melodic form

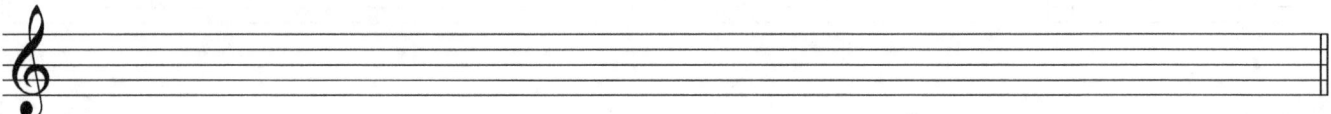

D natural minor

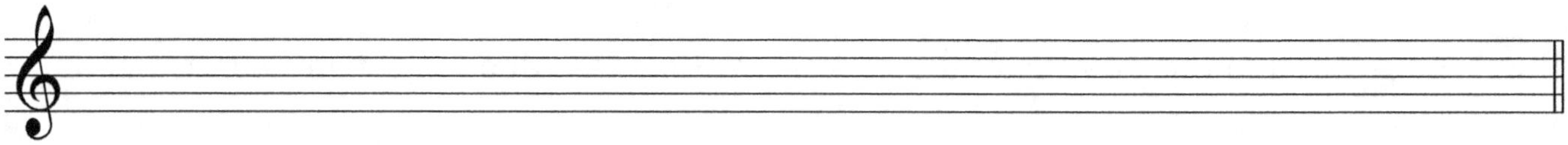

D minor's relative major

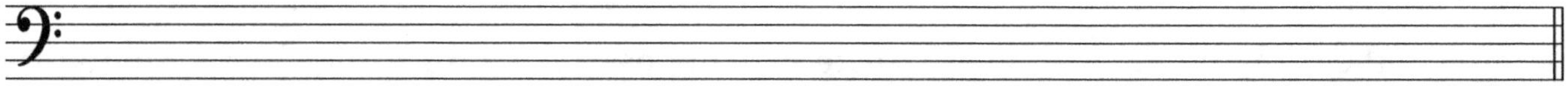

D minor's parallel major

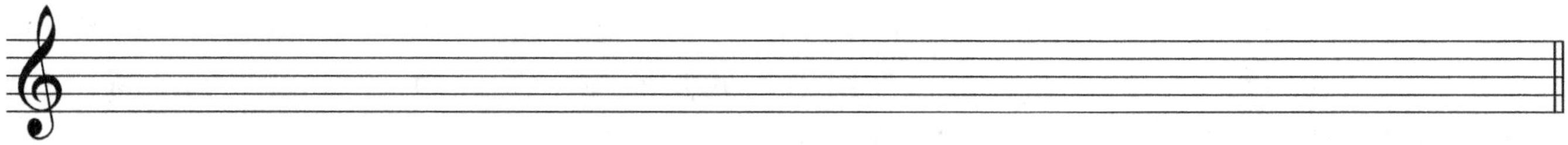

A major

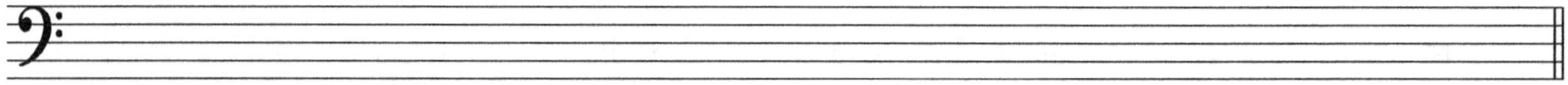

A major's parallel minor, melodic form

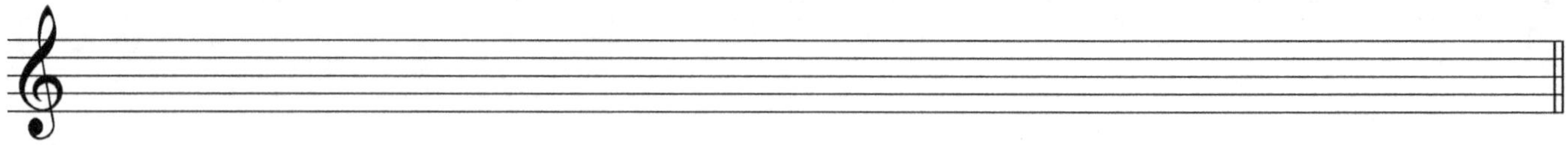

A major's relative minor, harmonic form

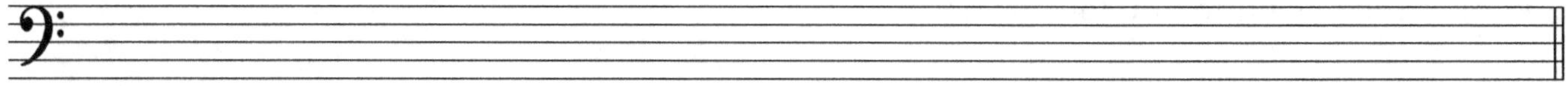

Identifying the Key of a Melody

It is important to know the key of a piece of music. Identifying the key of a composition helps us to understand, analyze, perform and memorize it.

Study the melody in Figure 5.6.

This melody has a key signature of one sharp. This key signature suggests G major or it's relative minor, E minor. This melody also has the accidental D sharp. Often, music in a minor key will have accidentals indicating raised $\hat{7}$. In the key of E minor raised $\hat{7}$ is D♯. This melody ends on E, approached by the leading tone D♯. There is an E minor arpeggio in m.4. All of these elements point to the key of E minor. This melody is in E minor.

Melodies in minor keys may contain raised $\hat{6}$ as well as raised $\hat{7}$ since the melodic minor scale includes these notes. In fact, a melody in a minor key could be based on any of the three forms of the minor scale: natural, harmonic, or melodic minor.

Figure 5.6

Felix Mendelssohn
Quartet No. 4

The melody is Figure 5.7 has a key signature of three sharps. This key signature suggests A major or it's relative minor, F♯ minor. The melody starts and ends on A. There are no E♯'s suggesting the raised $\hat{7}$ of F♯ minor. Therefore, it is in the key of A major.

Figure 5.7

Ludwig van Beethoven
Sonata no. 3 for Cello and Piano

1. Name the keys of the following melodies.

6
Intervals 1

Chromatic Half Steps

An *interval* can be defined as the distance from one note to the next. The smallest interval in the music we are studying is a half step.

Half steps may occur between two notes using the same letter name as shown in Figure 6.1. When a half step contains two notes with the same letter name, it is known as a ***chromatic half step***. For example, a chromatic half step above F is F♯. A chromatic half step below A is A♭. These half steps use the same letter name.

Study how sharps, flats, and naturals can raise or lower a note without changing its letter name.

Figure 6.1

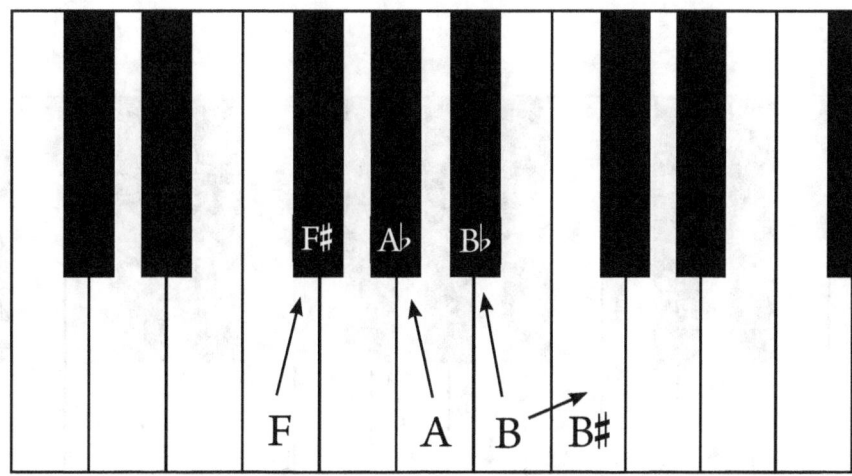

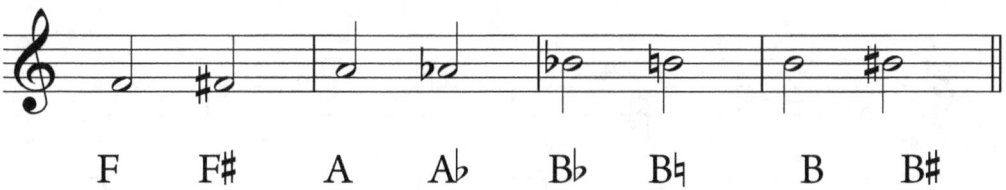

1. Write chromatic half steps above the following notes.

2. Write chromatic half steps below the following notes.

Diatonic Half Steps

Half steps may also occur between two notes with different letter names. Figure 6.2 shows half steps between notes using different letter names. When a half step contains two notes with different letter names it is known as a *diatonic half step*. The notes names occur in alphabetical order. For example, E♭ - F♭, F♯ - G, A - B♭, etc.

Figure 6.2

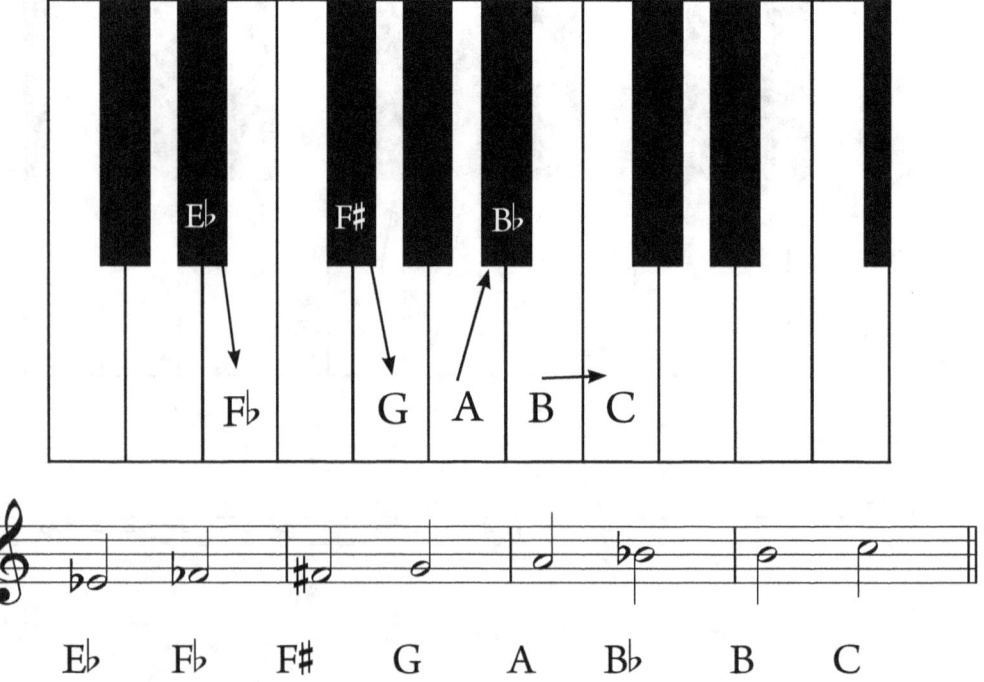

1. Write diatonic half steps above the following notes.

2. Write diatonic half steps below the following notes.

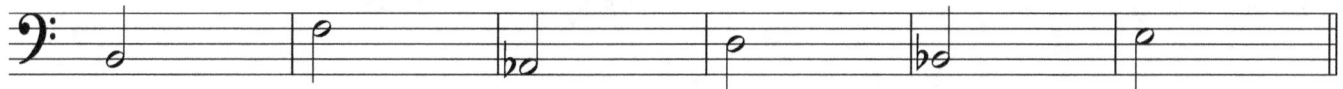

3. Name the following halfs steps as chromatic half steps (CHS) or diatonic half steps (DHS).

___ ___ ___ ___ ___ ___

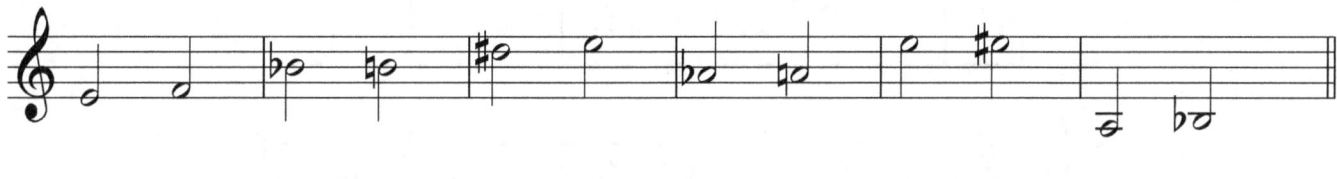

___ ___ ___ ___ ___ ___

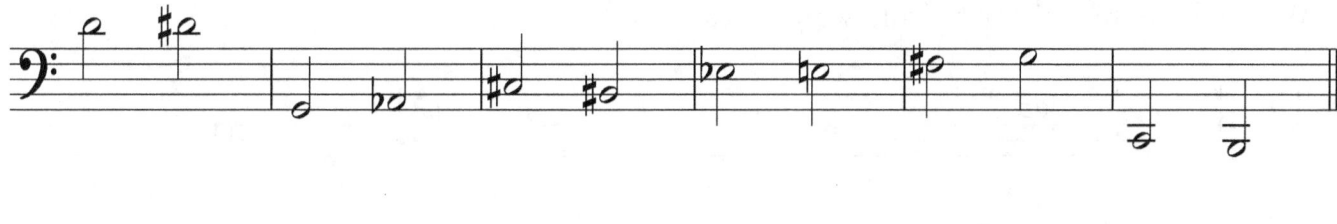

___ ___ ___ ___ ___ ___

___ ___ ___ ___ ___ ___

Whole Steps

A ***whole step*** is made up of two half steps. On the keyboard, there is always one key in the middle of a whole step. Sometimes the key is black, and sometimes it is white.

Figure 6.3 shows whole steps written on the score in music notation and where they occur on the keyboard. A whole step always contains two different letter names in alphabetical order. For example, F - G, A♭ - B♭, C♯ - D♯, or if it's a whole step below, D - C, B♭ - A♭, etc.

Figure 6.3

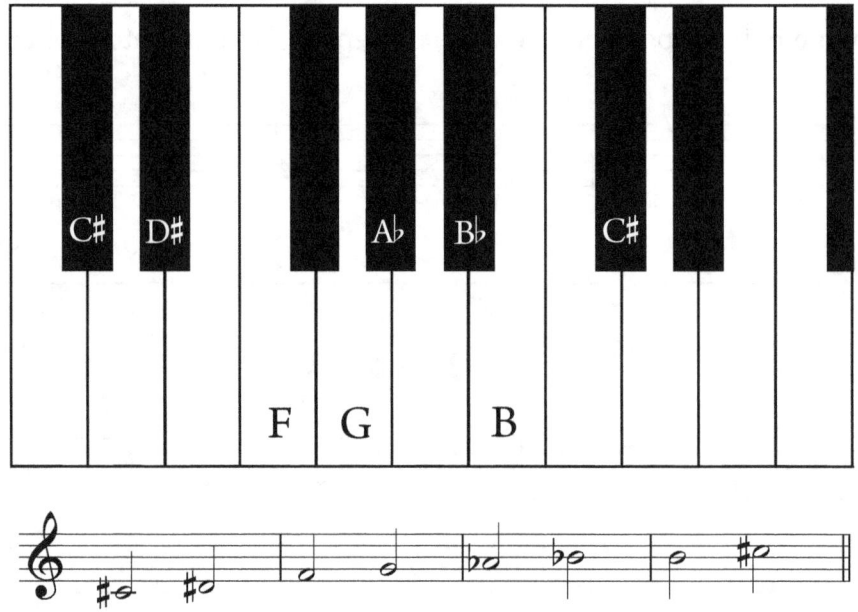

1. Write whole steps above the following notes.

2. Write whole steps below the following notes.

7

Intervals 2

Review

Major intervals use the numbers 2, 3, 6, and 7. Perfect intervals use 1, 4, 5, and 8. In order for an interval to be major or perfect the top note must be a member of the bottom notes major scale.

Figure 7.1 shows the major and perfect intervals formed between the notes of the C major scale.

Figure 7.1

1. The following notes are written above E♭ using the notes of the E♭ major scale. Name the number (2, 3, etc.) and quality of each interval (maj or per).

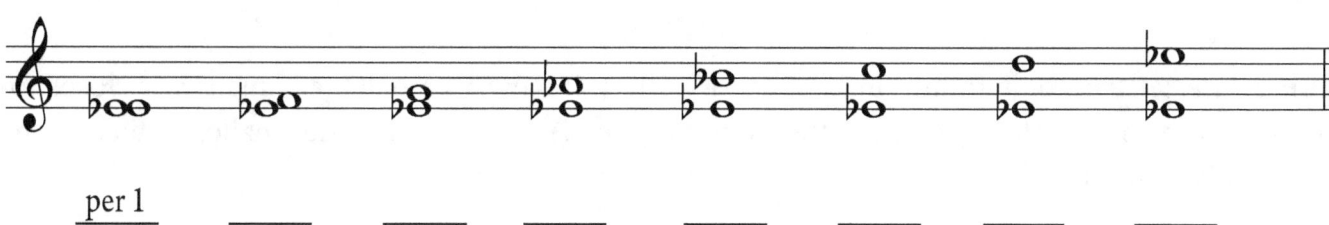

   per 1   ____   ____   ____   ____   ____   ____   ____

2. The following notes are written above A using the notes of the A major scale. Name the number (2, 3, etc.) and quality of each interval (maj or per).

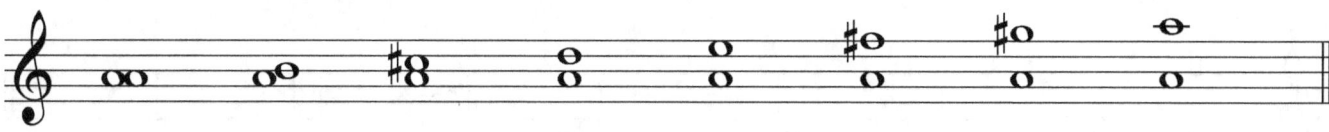

   ____   ____   ____   ____   ____   ____   ____   ____

3. Write each note of the A♭ major scale above each A♭ note. Name the size and quality of each interval.

___   ___   ___   ___   ___   ___   ___   ___

4. Write each note of the E major scale above each E note. Name the size and quality of each interval.

___   ___   ___   ___   ___   ___   ___   ___

Accidental Placement

When placing accidentals in front of intervals:

a. For interval numbers from 2 to 6, place the upper accidental closest to the note and the lower accidental to the left.
b. If the two accidentals of a 6th don't collide, they can be aligned vertically.
c. For an interval greater than a 6th, the intervals can align vertically.

Figure 7.2

Minor intervals are only found on 2, 3, 6, and 7. They are always a half step smaller or closer together than a major interval that has the same number. A minor 2nd is the smallest interval. The half step is a minor 2nd.

Figure 7.3 illustrates the differences between major and minor intervals. Lowering the top note of a major interval a half step creates a minor interval. Another way to create a minor interval is to raise the bottom note of a major interval. This brings the notes closer together by a half step.

Figure 7.3

maj 2   min 2   maj 3   min 3   maj 6   min 6   maj 7   min 7

1. Name the following major intervals. Rewrite them, making them minor, by lowering the top note one half step. Rename each interval. The first one is done for you.

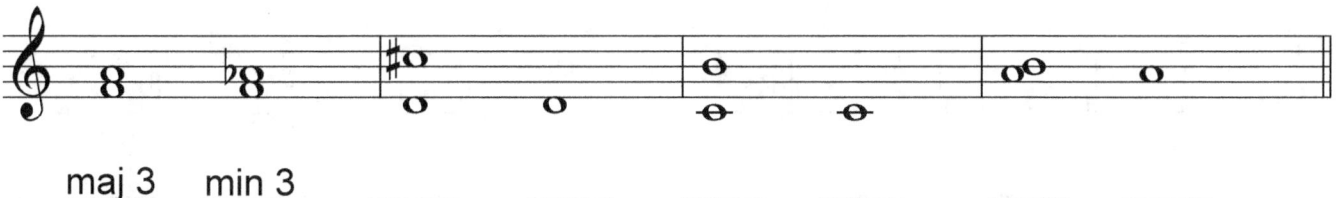

maj 3   min 3

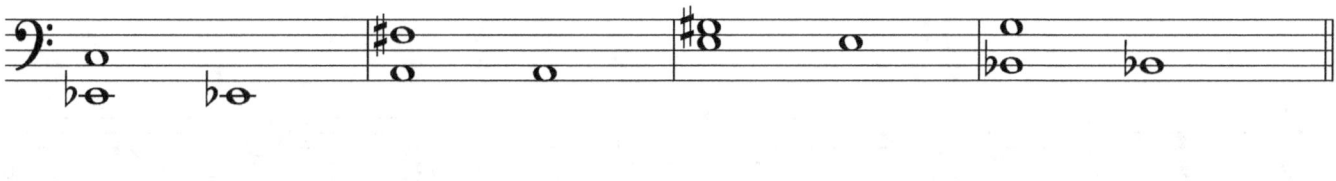

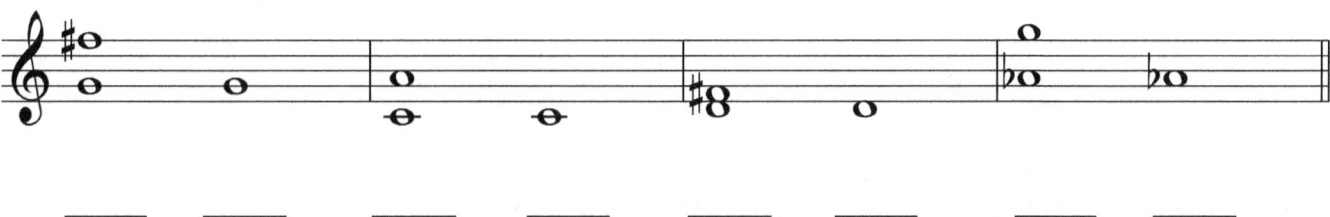

2. Name the intervals under the brackets.

Carl Maria von Weber
Der Freischutz

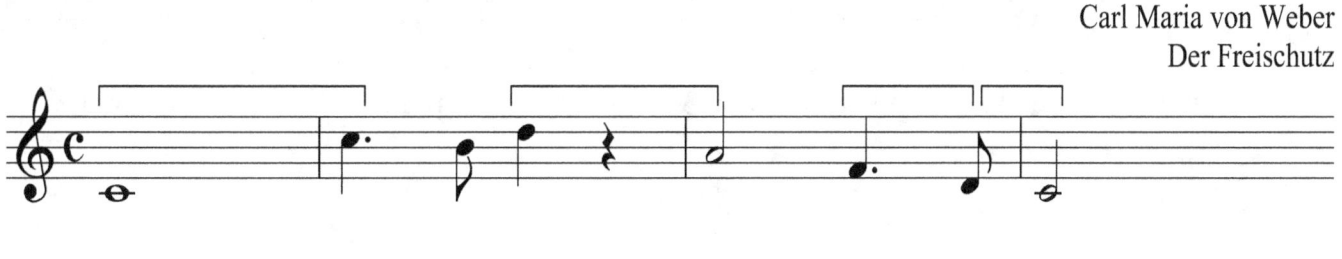

Ludwig van Beethoven
Sonata Op. 10 No. 2

3. Name the following intervals.

4. Write the following harmonic intervals above the given notes.

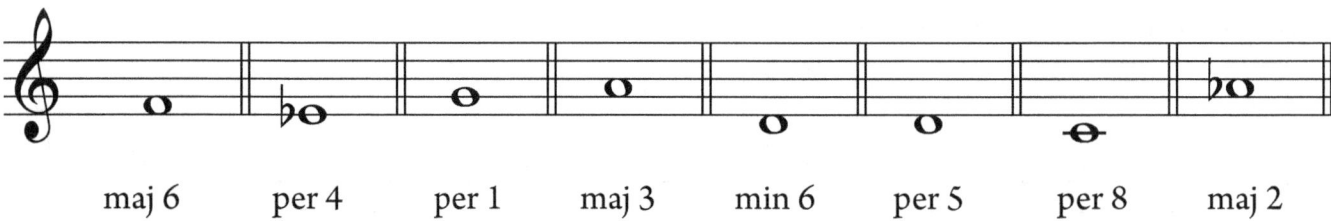

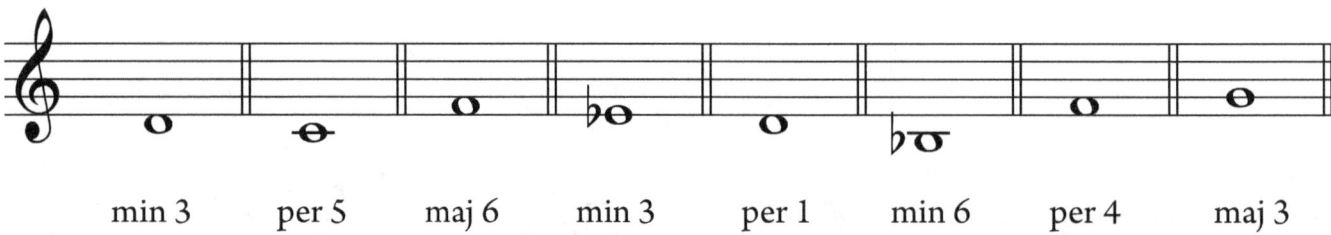

8
History 2

Wolfgang Amadeus Mozart (1756 - 1791) Classical Era

Wolfgang Amadeus Mozart was born in Salzburg, Austria, on January 27, 1756. He was born into a family of musicians and was an incredible child prodigy. Under the strong influence of his father, Mozart began composing music at the age of five! Here is a brief timeline of his life:

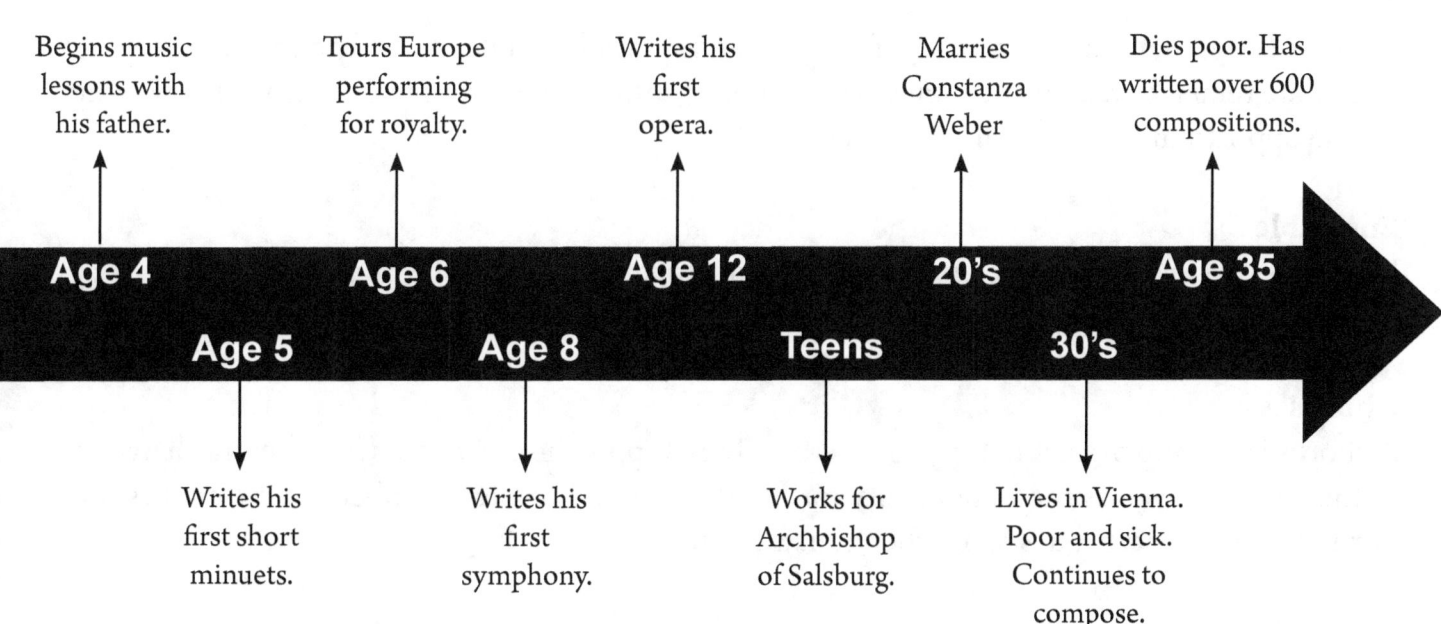

Opera

An *opera* is a play with music. The actual word "opera" is Italian for "work" and was first used in England in 1656. The earliest Italian operas were called favola in musica (fable in music) and drama per musica (drama by means of music).

The construction of an opera is like that of a play. It can be anywhere from one to five acts, and last anywhere from 30 minutes to five hours. The average opera is usually about 3 hours long. Like plays, operas are staged and use sets and costumes.

Operas usually begin with an *overture*. An overture is a piece of music played by the orchestra that contains melodies from the main part of the opera. The purpose of the overture is to inform the audience that the opera is starting and to set the mood.

Elements of an Opera

Here are some of the elements that are found in an opera:

Recitatives
Recitatives are simple melodies sung at the speed of normal speech. There were originally accompanied by a harpsichord, and in later operas, by the orchestra.

Arias
Arias are songs that can be taken out of an opera and sung as separate musical performances. Most operas are remembered for their finest arias. Arias are often challenging to perform, and give singers the opportunity to show off their voices.

Ensembles
Ensembles occur when characters in the opera sing together. They range from short duets to long, complex pieces involving many characters. Some of Mozart's ensembles can last for 20 minutes!

Choruses
A chorus is a group of singers, singing together. They supply the crowd scenes and extra characters in the opera, as well as the opportunity for beautiful choral music. Members of the chorus may portray servants, party guests, or other unnamed characters.

The Magic Flute (1791)

Mozart's famous opera, **The Magic Flute, Die Zauberflöte** in German, was composed in 1791. The **libretto** or text of the opera was written by Emanuel Schikaneder. It tells a fanciful and extraordinary story that includes a bird seller, a princess, a young prince who wants to rescue her, an evil Queen of the Night, a wise priest, and of course, a magic flute. The story is very complicated, but the music is beautiful and unforgettable.

The Magic Flute is a genre or type of opera called **Singspiel**. Singspiel (pronounced "zing-shpeel") originated in German-speaking countries and found its roots in comic opera. The translation of singspiel is "sing-play." It includes spoken dialogue between the singing, and often, an exotic or fanciful theme.

The Magic Flute is the most famous example of Singspiel. When Mozart was composing, opera was dominated by Italian traditions and language. Mozart decided to write this opera in German as a way to show pride and love of his country and culture and to connect with the common people, not just the elite. It contains a diverse cast of characters and some of Mozart's most magnificent music.

Music Terms

andantino	a little faster than andante
espressivo, espress.	expressive
larghetto	fairly slow, not as slow as largo
largo	very slow
pedale, ped.	pedal
rubato	flexible tempo with slight variations of speed to enhance musical expression.
spiritoso	spirited
tranquillo	tranquil

Queen of the Night Aria from "The Magic Flute"

"Der Hölle Rache kocht in meinem Herzen" ("Hell's vengeance boils in my heart"), is an aria sung by the Queen of the Night, in the second act of The Magic Flute. It is often called "The Queen of the Night Aria." In it, the Queen of the Night, who is in a tremendous rage, places a knife into the hand of her daughter Pamina and demands that she assassinate Sarastro, the Queen's rival.

The Queen of the Night is sung by a *coloratura soprano*. Sopranos sing in the highest range of the four voice parts. However, coloratura sopranos are capable of seemingly superhuman feats. In the Queen of the Night aria, the voice is extremely agile, firing out fast paced notes that ascend as high as the 3rd F above middle C. Coloratura soprano roles have existed from Baroque through 20th century opera.

An amazing performance of this aria by the gifted soprano Diana Damrau can be found on YouTube.

Figure 5.4 contains the opening measures of Der Hölle Rache kocht in meinem Herzen. The piano part is the orchestral reduction. The key is in D minor. **Allegro assai** means very fast.

Figure 5.4

Figure 5.5 shows the incredible virtuosity employed by the coloratura soprano in this aria.

Figure 5.5

This is the text for Der Hölle Rache kocht in meinem Herzen in German with English translation.

Der Hölle Rache kocht in meinem Herzen,	The vengeance of Hell boils in my heart,
Tod und Verzweiflung flammet um mich her!	Death and despair flame about me!
Fühlt nicht durch dich Sarastro Todesschmerzen,	If Sarastro does not through you feel The pain of death,
So bist du meine Tochter nimmermehr.	Then you will be my daughter nevermore.
Verstossen sei auf ewig,	Disowned may you be forever,
Verlassen sei auf ewig,	Abandoned may you be forever,
Zertrümmert sei'n auf ewig	Destroyed be forever
Alle Bande der Natur	All the bonds of nature,
Wenn nicht durch dich!	If not through you
Sarastro wird erblassen!	Sarastro becomes pale! (as death)
Hört, Rachegötter,	Hear, Gods of Revenge,
Hört der Mutter Schwur!	Hear a mother's oath!

Review 2

1. Write the following scales ascending and descending in whole notes using a key signature for each.

F major

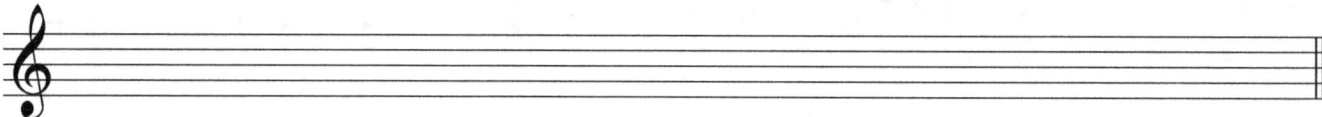

F major's parallel minor, harmonic form

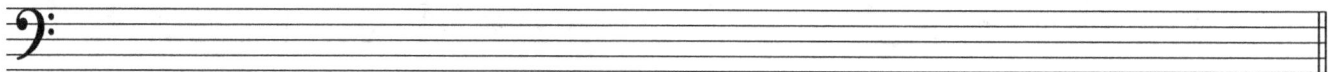

F major's relative minor, melodic form

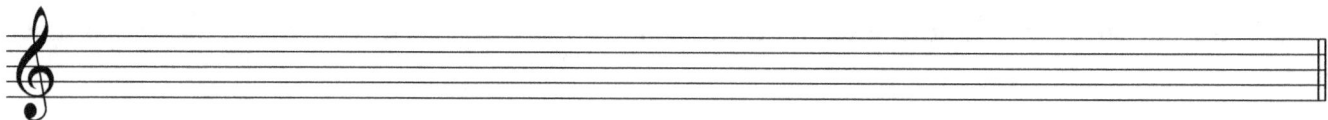

2. Name the following as chromatic half step (CHS), diatonic half step (DHS), or whole step (WS).

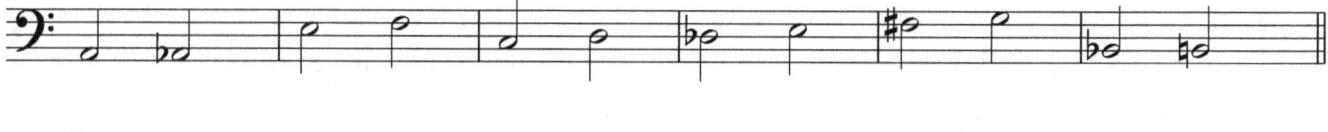

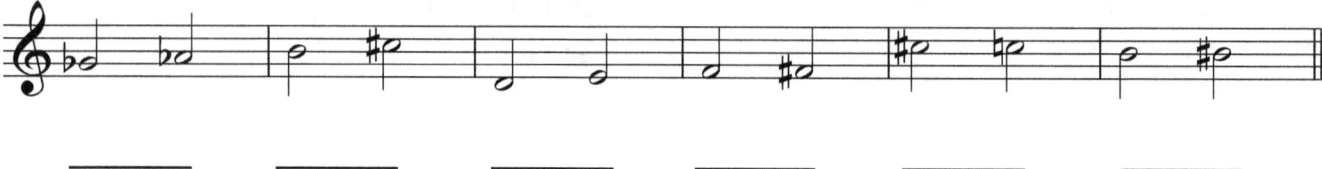

3. Write the following intervals above the given notes.

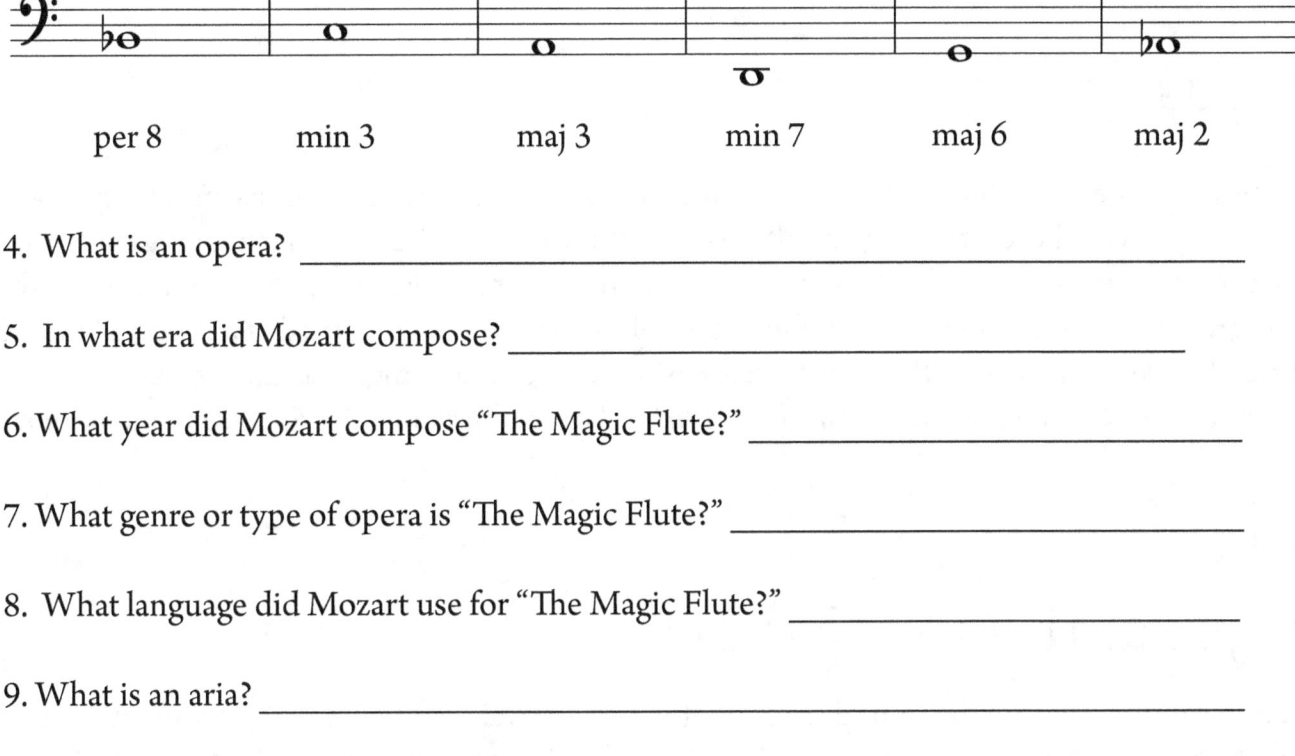

4. What is an opera? _____

5. In what era did Mozart compose? _____

6. What year did Mozart compose "The Magic Flute?" _____

7. What genre or type of opera is "The Magic Flute?" _____

8. What language did Mozart use for "The Magic Flute?" _____

9. What is an aria? _____
_____

10. What type of soprano sings the Queen of the Night aria? _____

11. Match the following terms with the correct definitions.

   _____*andantino*   a) expressive

   _____*espressivo, espress.*   b) a little faster than andante

   _____*larghetto*   c) very slow

   _____*largo*   d) fairly slow, not as slow as largo

9
Chords

Triads

Scales and intervals combine to form **chords**. Chords are the foundation of harmony. There are many types of chords, but they are all based on the same principles. Understanding the major scale can go a long way to understanding chords. In this lesson, we are going to continue our study of the **triad.** Chord is a general name for notes played together, and a triad is a specific kind of chord. The prefix "tri" means three. A tricycle has three wheels, a triangle has three sides, and a triad has three notes. Triads occur in various **qualities**. Two of these qualities are *major* and *minor*.

Major and Minor Triads

The notes of the triad are the root, third and fifth. The interval quality of the third and fifth determine the triad quality. Figure 9.1 contains a C major and a C minor triad. The ***major triad*** consists of the intervals of a major 3rd and perfect 5th above the root. The ***minor triad*** consist of the intervals of a minor 3rd and a perfect 5th above the root.

Figure 9.1

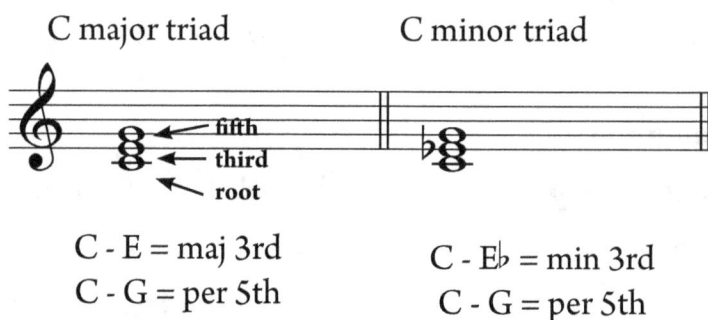

Triad Inversions

Root Position

The three notes of a triad can be placed in a different order within the chord. The lowest note of a triad is very important because it determines its position. If the lowest note is the root, the triad is in *root position*. This is the most common triad. The triads that we have studied so far have been in root position. The C triads in Figure 9.1 are in root position because the root C is the lowest note in each case.

First Inversion

Whenever another note of the triad is the lowest note, the triad is in **inversion**. A *first inversion triad* has the third as the lowest note. The order of the notes of the rest of the chord makes no difference. The bottom note determines the position.

Figure 9.2 contains the E♭ major triad in root positon and first inversion. When the 3rd of the triad (G) is the lowest note, the triad in in first inversion.

The chords have been named in two ways. The root/quality symbol for first inversion is **E♭/G**. This means that it is the E♭ major triad with G on the bottom. This method of naming chords is typical in popular music. The formula for this is triad/bass note.

The functional chord symbol is **I⁶**. "I" indicates that it is a major triad built on $\hat{1}$ in E♭ major and the "6" indicates that it is in first inversion. The origin of the 6 comes from the interval of a 6th between the lowest note G and the highest note E♭ in the triad.

Figure 9.2

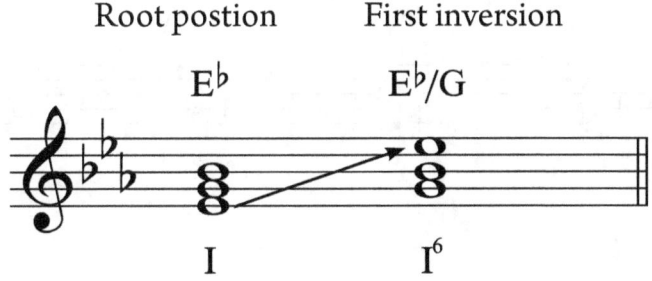

Second Inversion

When the fifth is the lowest note of a triad, it is in **second inversion.** Figure 9.3 contains the E♭ major triad in second inversion. The order of the remaining notes does not matter. The lowest note determines the position. Here, B♭, the fifth of the E♭ major triad is the bottom note making this triad second inversion.

The root/quality chord symbol is **E♭/B♭** indicating the E♭ major triad with B♭ as the lowest note. The functional chord symbol is **I $^6_4$** because the intervals above the lowest note are a 6th and a 4th.

Figure 9.3

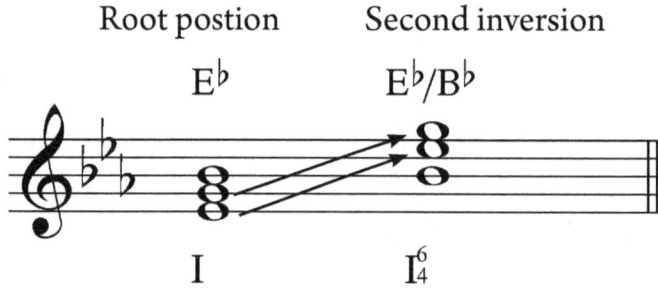

Minor Chord Symbols

The chord symbols for minor triads function in the same way as those for major triads with a few small differences. Figure 9.4 shows the chord symbols for minor triads. In root/quality chord symbols, minor triads are indicated with an "m" beside the uppercase letter. In functional chord symbols, minor triads are shown with a lower case Roman numeral.

Figure 9.4

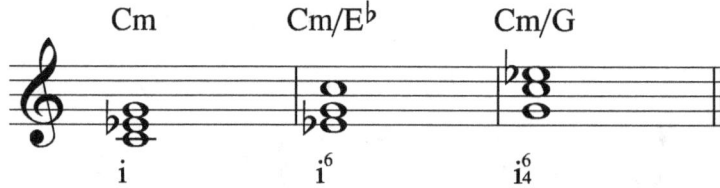

Accidental Placement

When placing accidentals in front of a triad, if there are two accidentals, the upper accidental goes closest to the note and the lower accidental is placed to the left.

If there are three accidentals, the upper accidental is placed closest to the note, the lower accidental is placed slightly to the left, and the middle accidental is placed even farther left.

Figure 9.5

1. Identify the following triads as major or minor. Write the root/quality chord symbols for each.

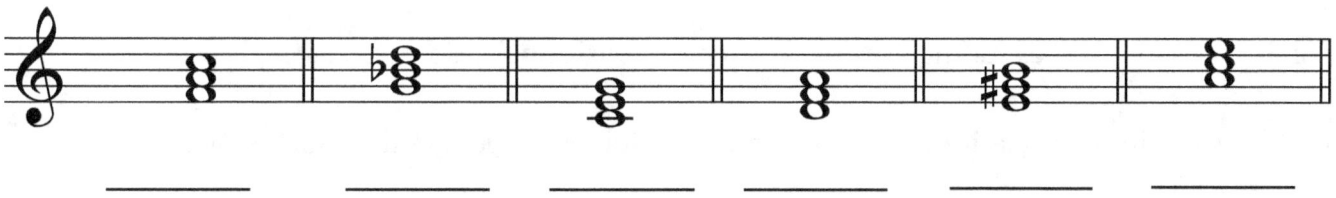

____ ____ ____ ____ ____ ____

____ ____ ____ ____ ____ ____

2. Write a major triad and its inversions using the following notes as the root. Write the root/quality chord symbols for each.

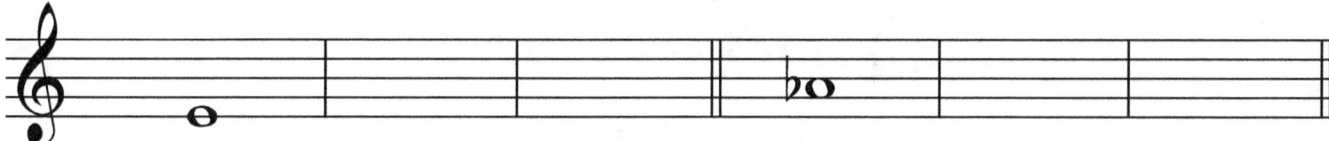

3. Write a minor triad and its inversions using the following notes as the root. Write the root/quality chord symbols for each.

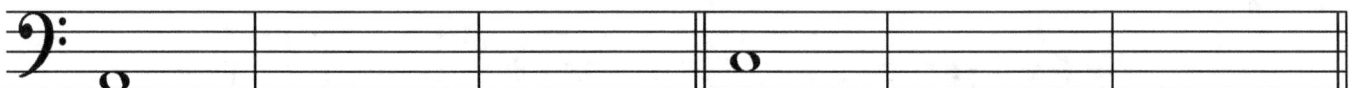

Solving Triads

Solving a triad involves stating its root, quality and position. To solve a triad:

1. If it is not in root position, put it into root position. For Figure 9.6 the root is: **E♭**.

Figure 9.6

2. Determine the intervals between the root and 3rd and the root and 5th. In Figure 9.7 E♭ to G is a major 3rd and E♭ to B♭ is a perfect 5th making its quality **major**.

Figure 9.7

E♭ - G = maj 3   E♭ - B♭ = per 5

3. Examine the lowest note of the given triad. In Figure 9.6 it is the 3rd, G. When the 3rd is the lowest note, the position of the triad is **first inversion**. This triad is solved as follows:

Root: E♭
Quality: major
Position: 1st inversion

1. Name the root of the following triads.

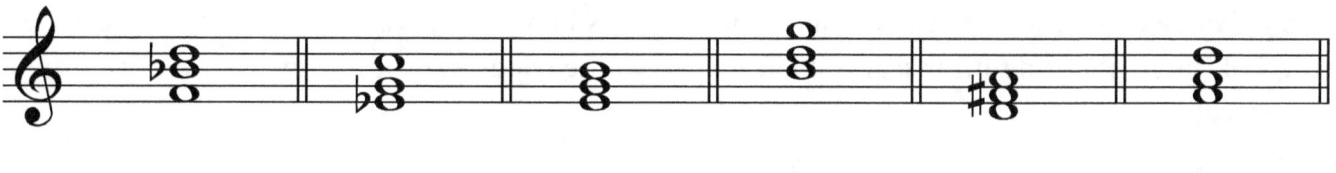

____ ____ ____ ____ ____ ____

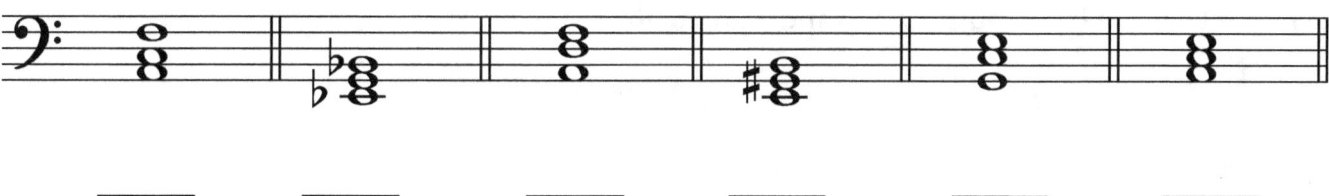

____ ____ ____ ____ ____ ____

2. Solve the following triads by stating the root, quality, and position.

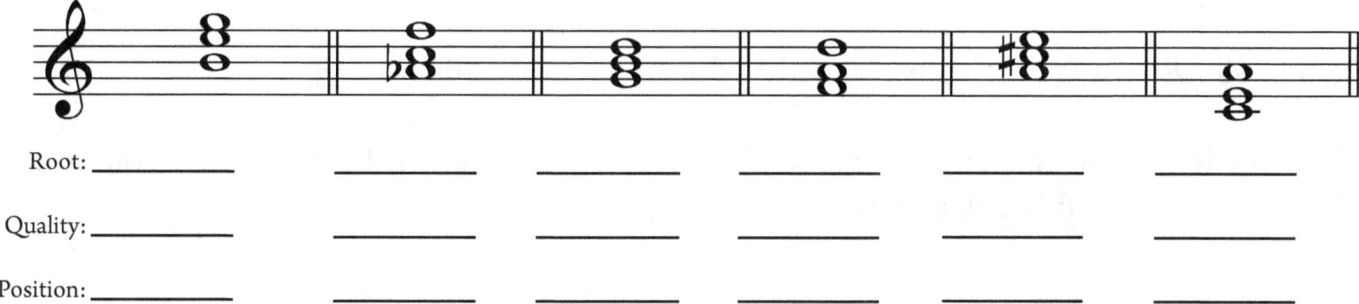

Root: _____ _____ _____ _____ _____ _____

Quality: _____ _____ _____ _____ _____ _____

Position: _____ _____ _____ _____ _____ _____

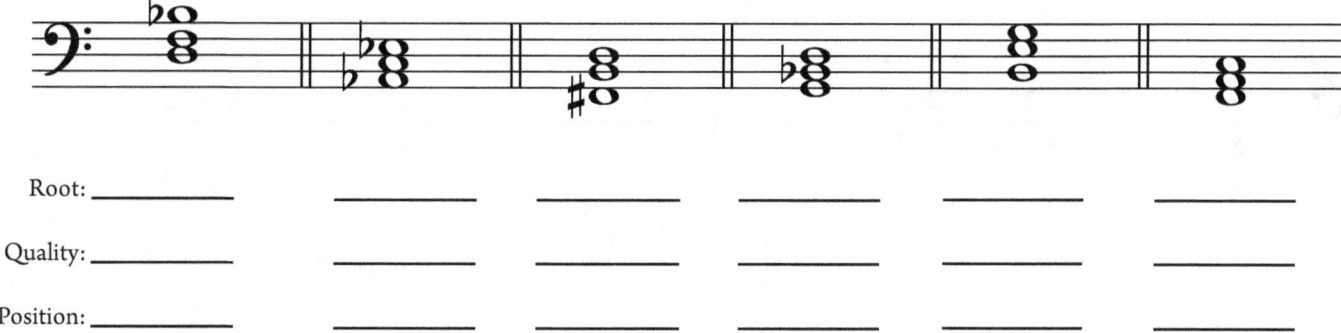

Root: _____ _____ _____ _____ _____ _____

Quality: _____ _____ _____ _____ _____ _____

Position: _____ _____ _____ _____ _____ _____

Primary Triads Built on Major and Minor Scales

The *primary triads,* which are the three central triads in any key, are built on scale degrees $\hat{1}$, $\hat{4}$, and $\hat{5}$ of the major and minor scale. Figure 9.8 shows the triads that occur on $\hat{1}$, $\hat{4}$, and $\hat{5}$ of the C major scale.

Each triad is named for the scale degree it is built upon. The triad built on $\hat{1}$, the tonic, is considered the *tonic triad.* The triad built on $\hat{4}$, the subdominant, is considered the *subdominant triad.* The triad built on $\hat{5}$ is the *dominant triad.*

In major keys the triads built on $\hat{1}$, $\hat{4}$ and $\hat{5}$ are major triads.

Figure 9.8

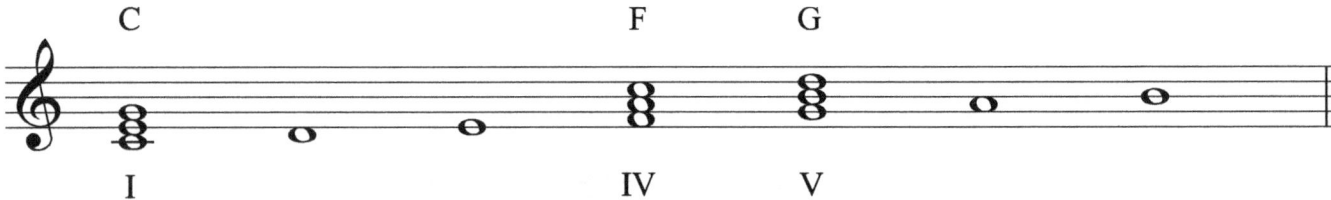

Figure 9.9 shows the triads built on $\hat{1}$, $\hat{4}$, and $\hat{5}$ of the A harmonic minor scale.

Minor triads occur on the tonic ($\hat{1}$) and subdominant ($\hat{4}$). A major triad occurs on the dominant ($\hat{5}$). The dominant triad contains raised $\hat{7}$.

Figure 9.9

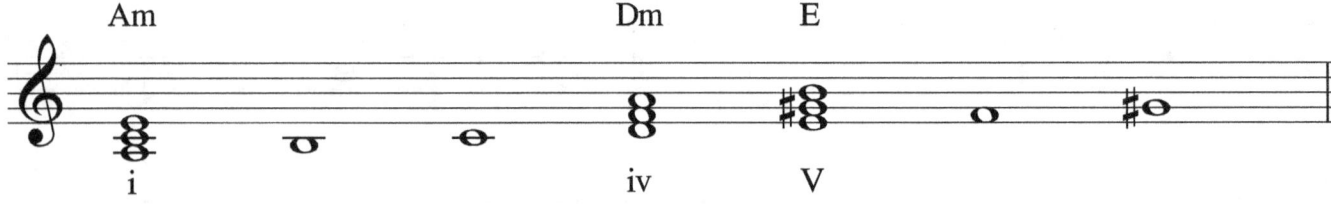

1. Build triads in the places indicated by Roman numerals on the following scales. Add the root/quality chord symbols above each triad.

D major

B♭ major

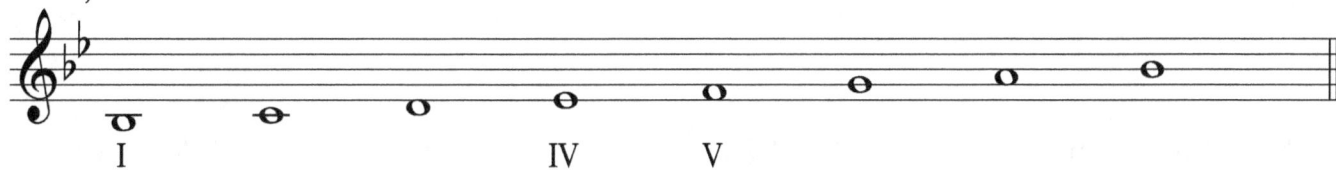

E minor

D minor

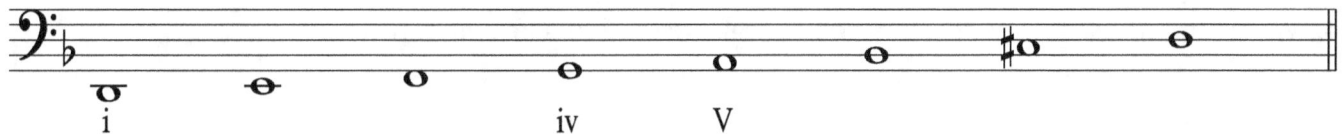

2. Write the following triads as indicated using a key signature for each. Add the root/quality chord symbol to each.

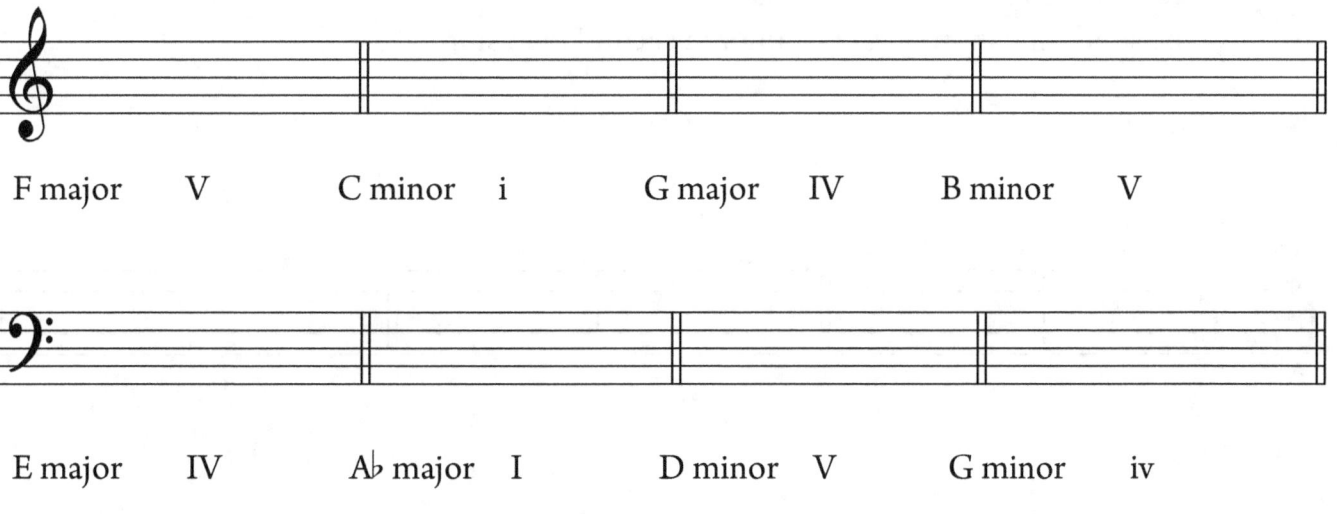

F major   V   C minor   i   G major   IV   B minor   V

E major   IV   A♭ major I   D minor   V   G minor   iv

Chords

3. Write the following triads using a key signature for each. Write the functional chord symbol.

| The tonic triad in F major | The dominant triad in C minor | The subdominant triad in B♭ major | The dominant triad in D minor |

| The subdominant triad in F minor | The tonic triad in E major | The dominant triad in B minor | The subdominant triad in A♭ major |

4. Write the following triads using accidentals instead of a key signature.

   a) the tonic triad of G minor in second inversion
   b) the dominant triad of D major in root position
   c) the subdominant triad of E minor in first inversion
   d) the dominant triad of C♯ minor in root position
   e) the tonic triad of E♭ major in first inversion
   f) the subdominant triad of F♯ minor in second inversion

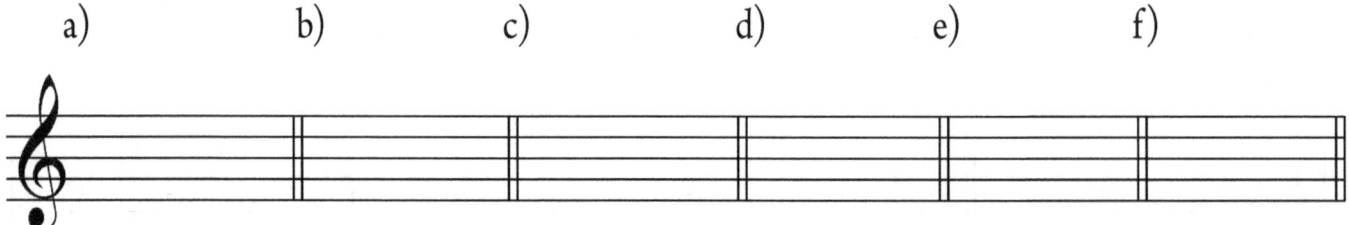

The Dominant Seventh Chord

Seventh chords are very common in Western music and we hear them all the time.

One of the most common seventh chords is the ***dominant seventh***. The functional chord symbol for the dominant seventh is V^7. This means that the chord is built on scale degree $\hat{5}$ (the dominant) and there is the interval of a seventh above the root of the chord. It contains four notes: the root, the 3rd, the 5th and the 7th. V^7 is a major triad with a minor 7th above the root. In other words, the intervals above the root are a major 3rd, perfect 5th and a minor 7th.

Figure 9.10 contains the dominant triad and the dominant seventh chord in C major. The root/quality chord symbol for V^7 is G^7.

Figure 9.10

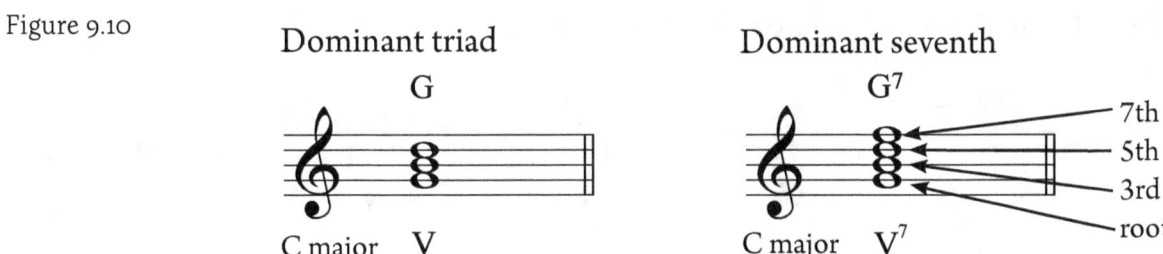

V^7 contains certain notes, like the leading tone, which pull our ear toward the tonic chord.

Figure 9.11 shows V^7 chords in C and G major and D and E minor. When we use a key signature for these chords, the seventh of V^7 is automatically a minor seventh. In minor keys V^7, like V needs a raised $\hat{7}$.

Figure 9.11

The dominant seventh sounds the same in tonic major and minor keys.

Figure 9.12 show the dominant seventh chords in F major and F minor. Even though the notation is different they sound the same and are made up of the same notes.

Figure 9.12

A Note About Terminology

The leading tone is the seventh degree of the scale. It may also be referred to as scale degree 7 ($\hat{7}$). We don't call the leading tone the "seventh." It is considered the *leading tone* or *scale degree seven* ($\hat{7}$). The word "seventh" is the term reserved to indicate the seventh of a seventh chord. In this case the word seventh may also be abbreviated to "7th."

The dominant 7th chord in C major is GBDF. F is the 7th of this chord. B, the 3rd of this chord, is the leading tone or scale degree $\hat{7}$ in C major. B is not called the *7th of C major*. The word "*seventh*" is reserved to indicate the 7th of a 7th chord.

1. Name the major key of the following dominant 7th chords.

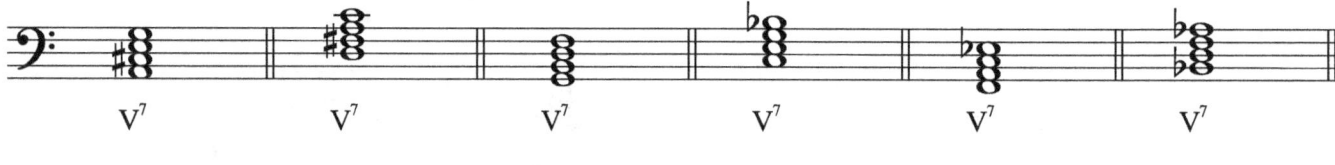

2. Each note below is the root of a dominant 7th chord. Build a dominant 7th chord above each by writing a major 3rd, perfect 5th and minor 7th above the root. Add the root/quality chord symbols above each chord.

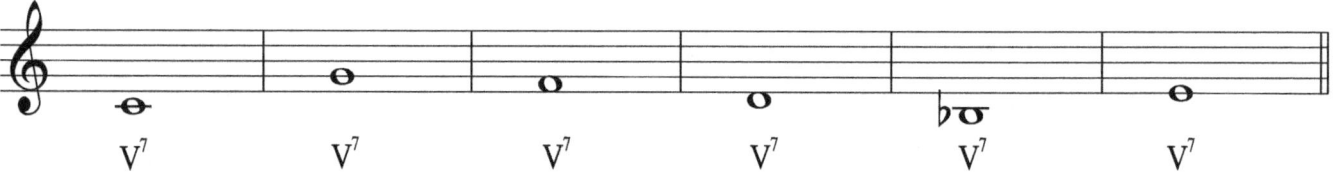

3. Write dominant 7th chords for the following keys. Use a key signature for each.

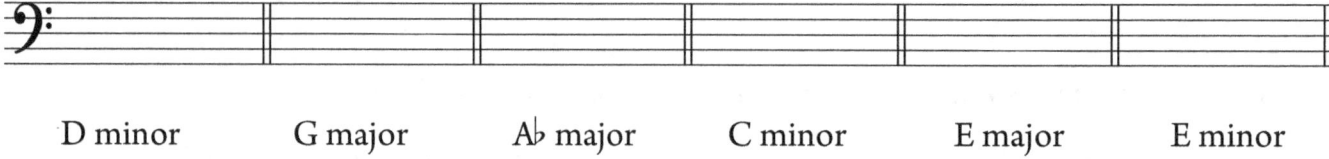

4. Write dominant 7th chords using a key signature according to the root/quality chord symbols. Name the **major key** for each.

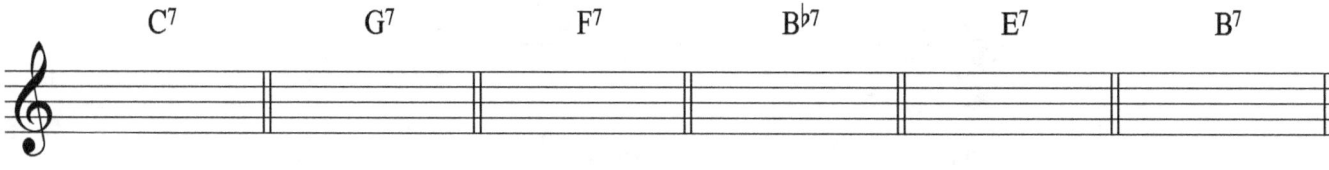

10
Octave Transposition

Transposition takes place when notes are moved up or down. The intervals between the notes remain the same.

In this level we are going to transpose by writing melodies at a different octave.

Figure 10.1 shows a short melody transposed up one octave from the bass clef into the treble clef.

Figure 10.1

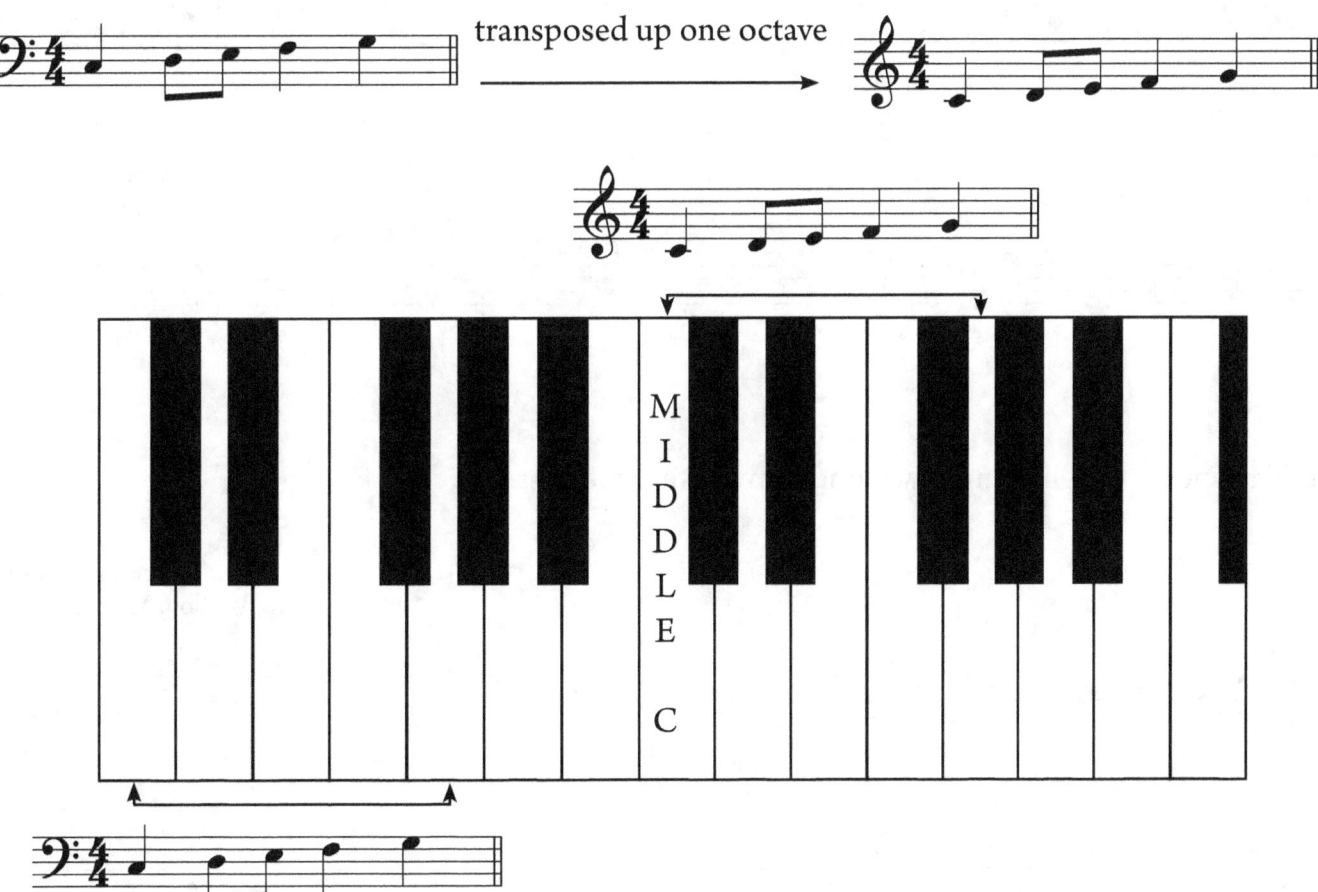

This is not the only way to transpose. Notes on the treble staff may be transposed down onto the bass staff.

The melody in Figure 10.2 is transposed down one octave from the treble staff to the bass staff.

When you transpose by an octave:

1. The key remains the same. The clef changes, but you use the same key signature (written correctly for the new clef).
2. The time signature remains the same.
3. Every note moves the interval of a perfect octave.
4. The normal rules of stem direction are followed.

This melody requires quite a few ledger line notes on the bass staff to obtain the correct pitch.

Figure 10.2

1. Transpose the following down one octave using the bass clef.

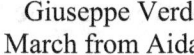

2. Transpose the following up one octave using the treble clef.

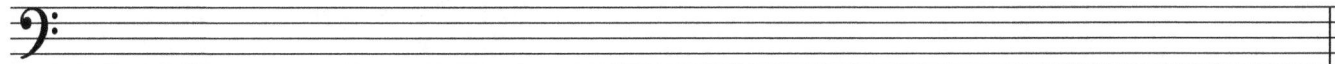

Octave Transposition

3. Rewrite the following melodies at the same pitch in the bass clef.

4. Rewrite the following melodies at the same pitch in the treble clef.

11

Melody Writing

The Motive

Many phrases are built from smaller groups of notes called ***motives***. A motive is a specific pattern of notes and rhythms. Motives can be repeated at a higher or lower pitch.

Figure 11.1 contains a melodic motive in m.1 consisting of a half note, two eighths and a quarter. It skips up a 3rd and then steps down. In the two measures that follow, the motive is repeated a step higher each time.

Figure 11.1

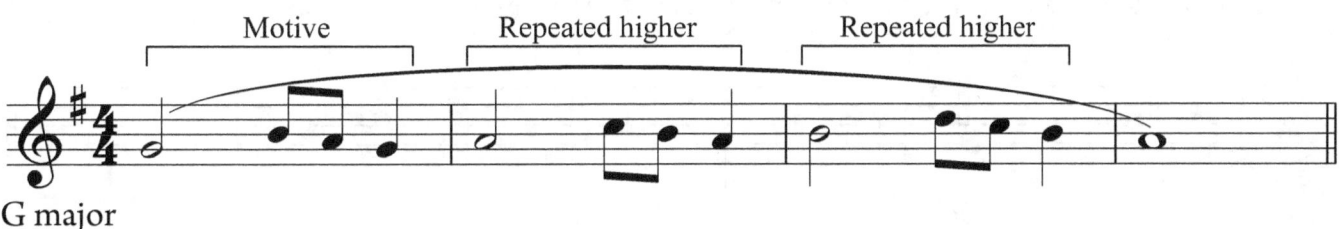

G major

Figure 11.2 contains the famous motive from the first movement of Beethoven's Fifth Symphony (Op. 67). The opening four note motive in mm.1 and 2 is repeated down a step in mm.3 and 4. This motive consists of an eighth rest followed by 3 eighth notes and a half note the interval of a 3rd lower. Beethoven based the majority of this large composition on this 4 note motive.

Figure 11.2

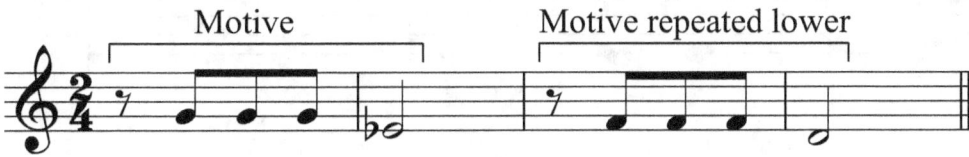

1. Name the major key of each of the following melodies. Circle the melodic motive each time it occurs in each melody.

key:

key:

key:

2. Name the key and find and circle the motives in the following melodies.

key:

key:

key:

Stable and Unstable Pitches

The strongest and most *stable pitch* of any key is the tonic ($\hat{1}$). A stable pitch is a note that has strength, finality, and completeness. Many melodies begin and end on the tonic. Another stable pitch is $\hat{3}$. $\hat{1}$ and $\hat{3}$ are the two most important notes of the tonic triad.

Some pitches within a key are considered **unstable**. An unstable pitch is a note that lacks finality or completeness. A composition would not end on an unstable pitch, but a phrase might. Unstable pitches are found on scale degrees $\hat{2}$ and $\hat{7}$. If scale degree $\hat{1}$ is like a period at the end of a sentence, scale degree $\hat{2}$ or $\hat{7}$ is like a question mark.

The melody in Figure 11.3 ends on scale degree $\hat{7}$. This is an unstable pitch and does not give us a sense of finality or completeness. Play this phrase and listen to this quality.

Figure 11.3

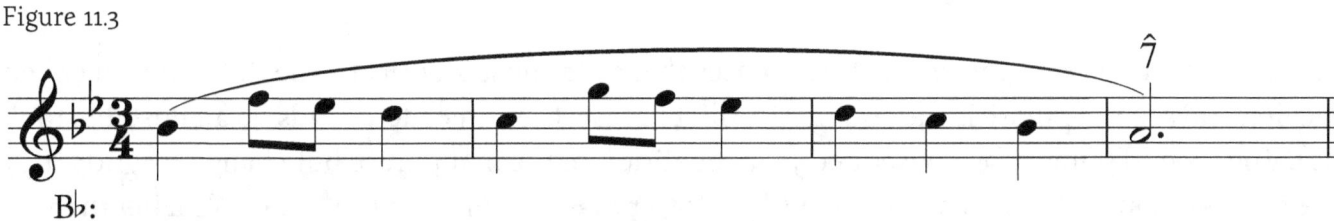

1. Name the major key of each melody. Write the scale degree number for the last note and mark it as stable or unstable.

Form: Antecedent and Consequent Phrases

Every piece of music has an overall plan or structure, which is the "big picture". This is called the *form* of the music.

Antecedent and **consequent** (question and answer) phrases are common in music. The antecedent phrase acts as a question, often ending on an unstable tone ($\hat{2}$ or $\hat{7}$), which requires an answer. The consequent phrase provides the answer to the antecedent phrase and usually ends on a stable tone ($\hat{1}$ or $\hat{3}$).

We can label music with letters to distinguish the differences within a piece. In this lesson we are going to look at melodies consisting of two phrases, and learn to identify their form and label them with letters.

The melody in Figure 11.5 consists of two phrases that are almost identical. The difference between the first and second phrase is the ending. The first phrase, the antecedent, ends on an unstable tone ($\hat{2}$). The second phrase, the consequent, is a repetition of the first phrase but changes slightly near the end and concludes on a stable tone ($\hat{1}$). Both phrases are nearly the same. We label the first phrase with the letter "**a**." The second phrase is very similar but not exactly the same, so we label it "**a¹**."

Since both phrases are very similar, they form a melodic idea called a ***parallel period***.

Figure 11.5

The two phrases in the melody in Figure 11.6 are different. Unlike the previous example the second phrase is not a repeat of the first with a different ending, but a completely new musical idea. In this case, we label phrase one "**a**" and phrase two "**b**". The two phrases work together to create a complete section. However, they are different melodically and the labels indicate the difference.

Since the two phrases use melodies that are different they form an idea called a ***contrasting period***.

Figure 11.6

1. Name the key of the following melody. Mark the phrases. Label the first phrase with the letter **a**. Label the second phrase with the letter **a¹** or **b** to show whether it is similar or different. Circle melodic motive 1 each time it occurs in the melody.

key:

The first phrase ends on: ❏ a stable scale degree   ❏ an unstable scale degree

The second phrase ends on: ❏ a stable scale degree   ❏ an unstable scale degree

This is a: ❏ parallel period   ❏ contrasting period

2. Name the key of the following melody. Mark the phrases. Label the first phrase with the letter **a**. Label the second phrase with the letter **a¹** or **b** to show whether it is the same or different.

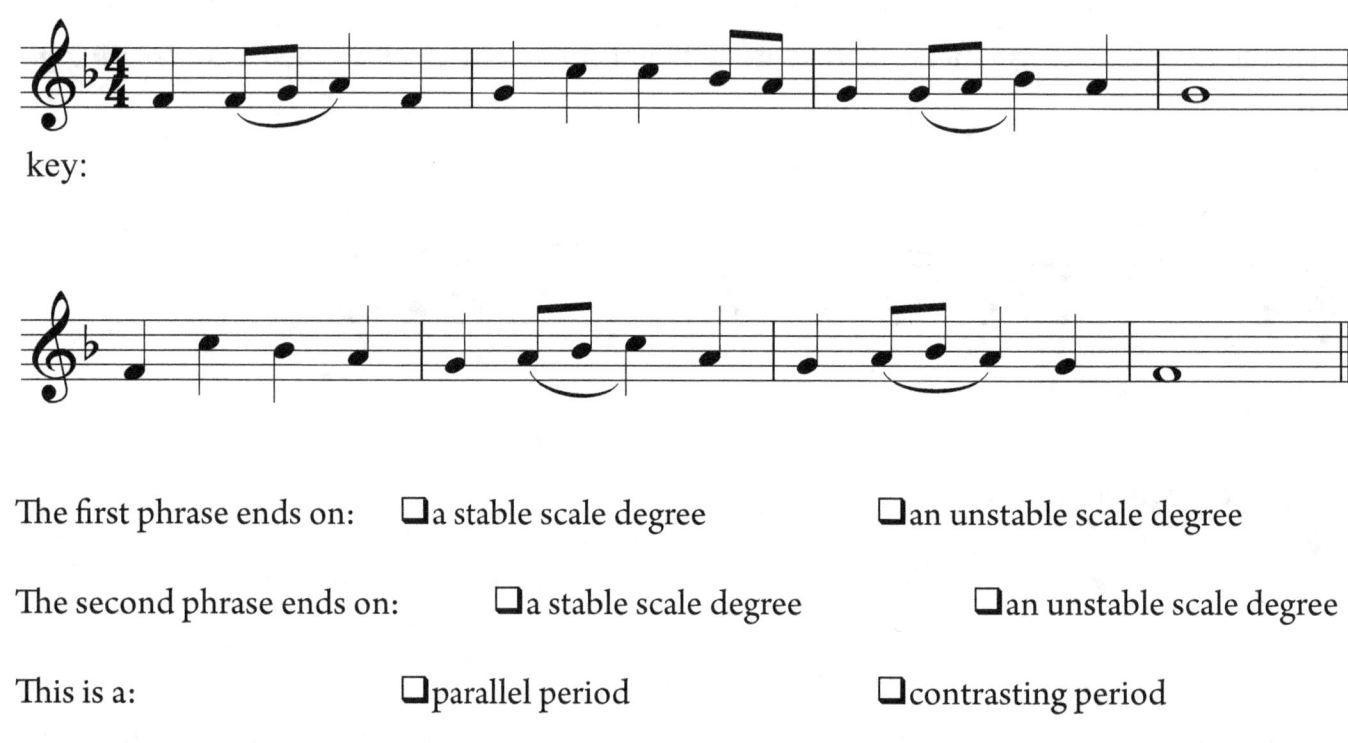

key:

The first phrase ends on: ❏ a stable scale degree   ❏ an unstable scale degree

The second phrase ends on: ❏ a stable scale degree   ❏ an unstable scale degree

This is a: ❏ parallel period   ❏ contrasting period

Composing a Consequent Phrase to a Given Melody

You may be asked to create a parallel period by composing a 4 measure consequent or answer phrase to a given melody. Here are the steps for writing this melody.

1. Examine the given melody and decide the key. The melody in Figure 11.7 is in F major.
2. Look at the last note of the phrase. Is it an stable or unstable scale degree? Here, it is $\hat{2}$, an unstable degree.

Figure 11.7

3. Since we are writing a parallel period we want the new phrase to begin the same way as the original phrase. Rewrite the opening phrase and change the ending so it ends on a stable scale degree ($\hat{1}$ or $\hat{3}$). Scale degree $\hat{1}$ is the strongest choice and is especially good if it is approached from a step below ($\hat{7}$-$\hat{1}$), or from a step above ($\hat{2}$-$\hat{1}$). Measure 3 of Figure 11.8 uses the same rhythm as the first two measures. This is good because it provides rhythmic unity. Try not to introduce a new or unusual rhythm when writing these phrases. This phrase concludes by stepping down to scale degree $\hat{1}$.

Figure 11.8

1. Create a parallel period by writing a 4 measure answer to the given question phrase. End your melody on a stable tone ($\hat{1}$ or $\hat{3}$). Mark the phrases.

key:

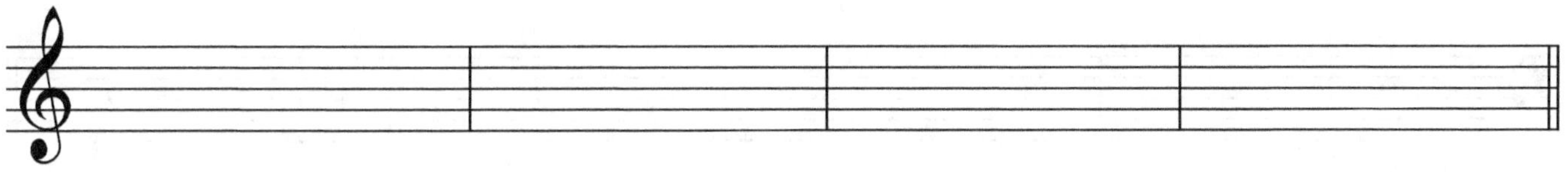

key:

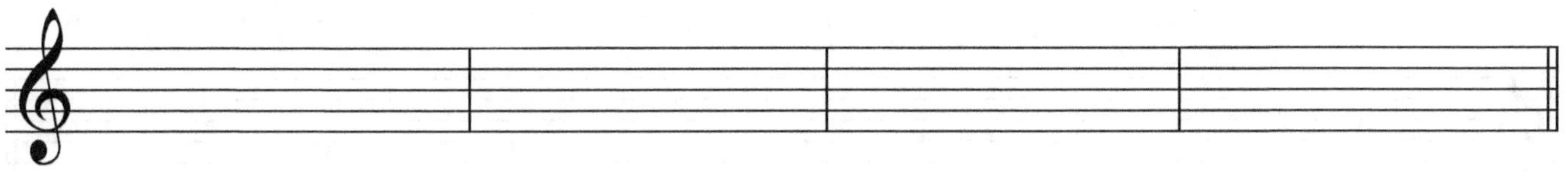

12
Form and Analysis

Answer questions dealing with the following musical excerpts.

1. Who composed the music shown above? _____

2. What is the name of the composition? _____

3. What key is it in? _____

4. What four voices are used to sing this piece?
   _____   _____   _____   _____

5. Name the triad formed by the notes at A _____

6. Name the interval at B. _____

7. Name the interval at C. _____

8. Name the interval at D. _____

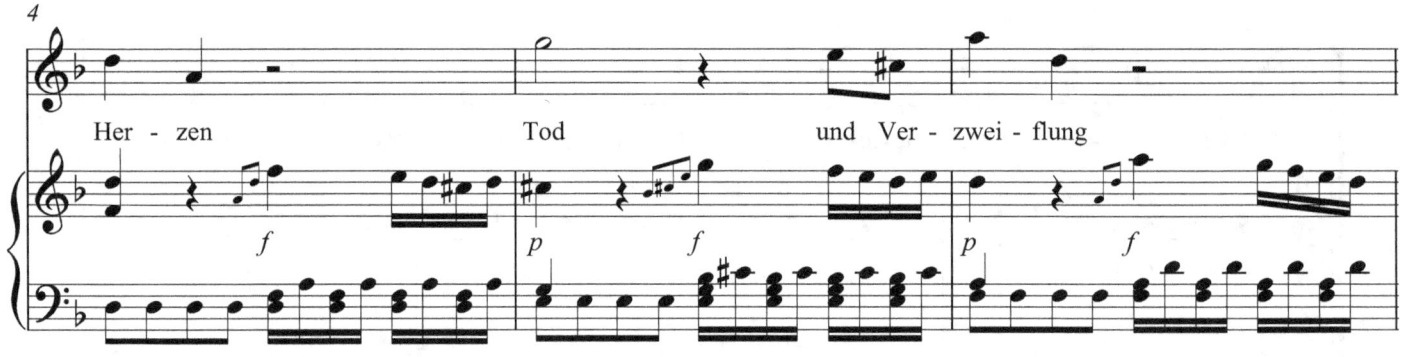

1. Who wrote the above musical example? _____

2. What musical period was it written? _____

3. What character is singing in this passage? _____

4. In what language is she singing? _____

5. What is the key of this piece? _____

6. Name the triad and inversion at A: _____
   B: _____
   C: _____

7. Circle one chromatic half step on the score. Label it CHS.

8. Define Allegro assai: _____

9. How many measures are in this example? _____

Sonatina

Cornelius Gurlitt
1820 -1901

1. Name the composer of this piece? _____

2. Name the key of this piece. _____

3. Write the time signature on the score.

4. Define "moderato" _____

5. How many phrases are in this example? _____

6. Does the first phrase end on a stable or unstable degree? _____

7. Does the second phrase end on a stable or unstable degree? _____

8. Label the phrases either: (a - a¹⁾) or (a - b) depending on the form.

9. What triad is formed by the notes in the box at letter A: _____

10. What triad is formed by the notes in the box at letter B: _____

11. Find the interval of a melodic minor 3rd, circle it, and label it min 3.

12. Find the interval of a melodic perfect 5th, circle it, and label it per 5.

13. Find two different diatonic semitones, circle them, and label them DS.

14. How many slurs occur in this piece? _____

Form and Analysis

Muzio Clementi
1752 -1832

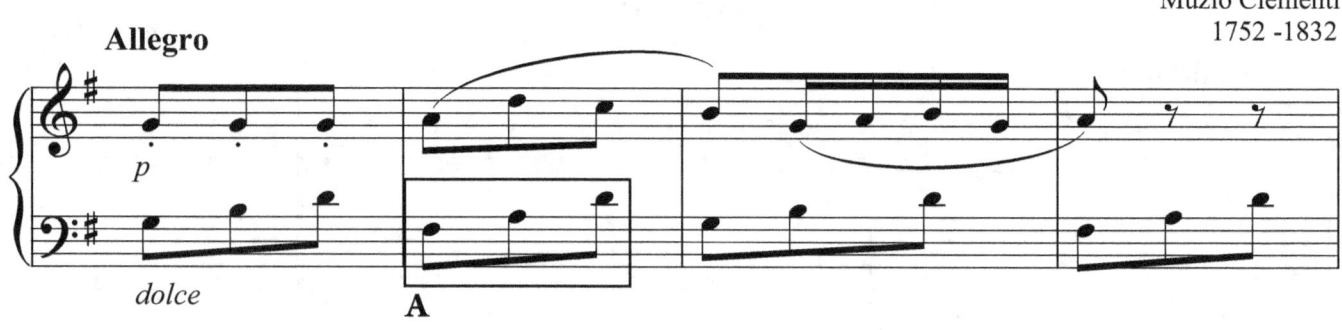

1. Name the composer of this piece? _____

2. When did he live? _____

3. Write the time signature on the score.

4. Name the key of this piece. _____

5. Define "allegro." _____

6. Define "dolce." _____

7. For the triad at letter A, name the: Root _____ Quality _____ Position _____

8. For the triad at letter B, name the: Root _____ Quality _____ Position _____

9. How many times does the broken tonic triad occur in the bass clef. _____

10. Find a melodic major 2nd, circle it and label it maj 2.

11. Find a melodic major 3rd, circle it and label it maj 3.

12. Find a diatonic half step, put a box around it and label is DHS.

©San Marco Publications 2022   Form and Analysis

1. Name the key of this piece? _____

2. Write the time signature on the score.

3. Check the terms that apply to this time signature. ❏compound   ❏triple   ❏simple   ❏duple

4. Mark the phrases with a slur.

5. Label each phrase using the letters *a*, *a¹* or *b*.

6. Define "andantino."_____

7. Name the triad at letter A.   root: _____   quality:_____

13
History 3

Harold Arlen (1905- 1986) Modern Era

Harold Arlen was an American composer, arranger, pianist, and vocalist. He worked as a piano accompanist in vaudeville during his early twenties. His first hit song "Get Happy" was composed with Ted Koehler in 1929.

In the 1930's and 40's, Arlen wrote some of his greatest hits including the score to the movie, The Wizard of Oz. He and his co-writer won the 1939 Academy Award for Best Original Song for "Over the Rainbow."

Stormy Weather, It's Only a Paper Moon, and I've Got the World on a String, are just a few of the standards that live on today and make Harold Arlen one of the most celebrated American composers of the 20th Century.

Over the Rainbow

Harold Arlen composed "Over the Rainbow," with lyricist Edgar Yipsel Harburg, for the 1939 movie The Wizard of Oz.

In the movie, it is sung by actress and singer Judy Garland who plays the role of Dorothy Gale. This film introduced Garland's powerful voice to the public. Visit YouTube for a recording of Garland's performance. Over the Rainbow is written for solo voice and orchestra. It follows a type of song form called AABA song form. This was a standard form used during the first part of the 20th century by composers like Harold Arlen, George Gershwin, and Irving Berlin. AABA songs are usually 32 bars in length and preceded by an Introduction.

AABA song form contains an opening section (A), a bridge (B), and a final A section. It is used in a variety of music genres including pop, jazz, and gospel.
The typical AABA song form follows this outline:

(Introduction)   **A** = 8 bars   **A** = 8 bars   **B** = 8 bars   **A** = 8 bars

AABA has no separate chorus, and the title usually appears at the beginning of each A section. In Over the Rainbow, each A section begins with the lyrics "Somewhere Over the Rainbow." The B section is contrasting and brings the listener back to the last A section.

The lyrics to Over the Rainbow help to illustrate the AABA song structure form.

Introduction	When all the world is a hopeless jumble, and the raindrops tumble all around, heaven opens a magic lane.
	When all the clouds darken up the skyway, There's a rainbow highway to be found, Leading from your window pane.
	To a place behind the sun, Just a step beyond the rain.
A	Somewhere over the rainbow, way up high, There's a land that I dreamed of, Once in a lullabye.
A	Somewhere over the rainbow, skies are blue, And the dreams that you dare to dream, Really do come true.
B	Someday day I'll wish upon a star, and wake up where the clouds are far behind me. Where troubles melt like lemon drops, Away above the chimney tops, That's where you'll find me.
A	Somewhere over the rainbow, skies are blue, And the dreams that you dare to dream, Really do come true. If happy little bluebirds fly. Beyond the rainbow, Why, oh why can't I?

Review 3

1. Name the Root, quality and position for the following triads.

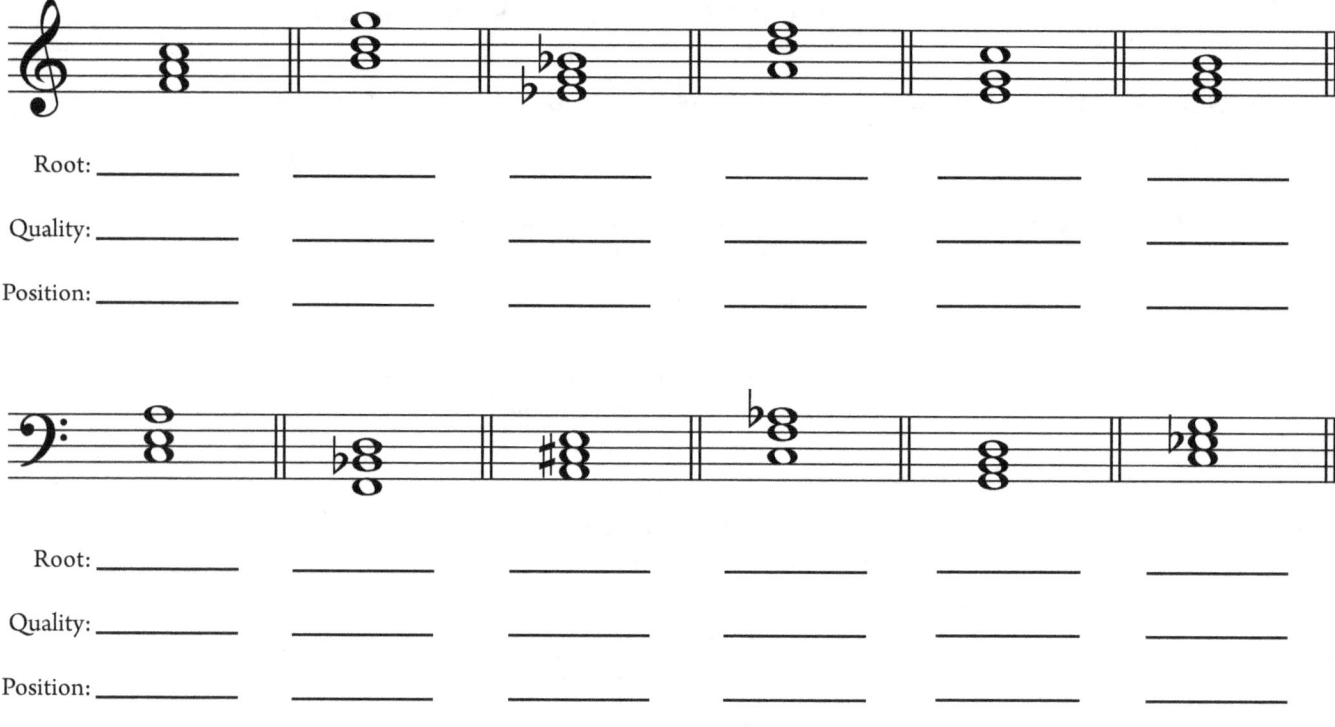

Root: _____ _____ _____ _____ _____ _____

Quality: _____ _____ _____ _____ _____ _____

Position: _____ _____ _____ _____ _____ _____

Root: _____ _____ _____ _____ _____ _____

Quality: _____ _____ _____ _____ _____ _____

Position: _____ _____ _____ _____ _____ _____

2. Write dominant 7th chords for the following keys. Use a key signature for each.

G minor   F major   A♭ major   D minor   E♭ major   C♯ minor

3. Match the following terms with the correct definitions.

____*spiritoso* a) pedal

____*tranquillo* b) flexible tempo with slight variations of speed to enhance musical expression.

____*pedale, ped.* c) spirited

____*rubato* d) tranquil

4. Transpose the following up one octave using the treble clef.

Franz Schubert
Waltz, Op. 50

5. Complete the following question phrase by writing an answer phrase. Mark the phrases. Label them as a, a¹, or b.

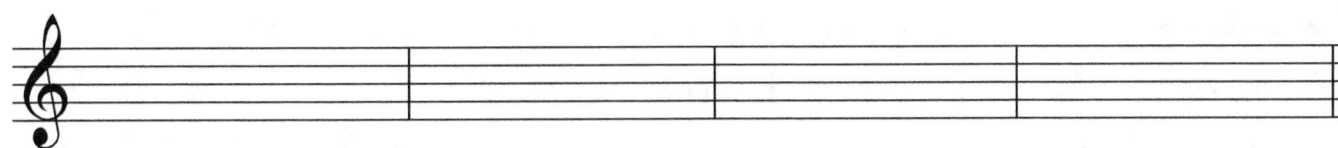

6. Choose the correct answer.

The composer of the Wizard of Oz:

❏ Harold Arlen ❏ George Gershwin ❏ Irving Berlin

Harold Arlen was:

❏ French ❏ Russian ❏ American

"Over the Rainbow" was written for:

❏ Bette Davis ❏ Judy Garland ❏ Beyonce

The song form of "Over the Rainbow" is:

❏ AABA ❏ ABBA ❏ ABAB

Music Terms and Signs

Terms

accelerando, accel.	becoming quicker
accent	a stressed note
adagio	slow
allegretto	fairly fast, a little slower than allegro
allegro	fast
andante	moderately slow, at a walking pace
andantino	a little faster than andante
a tempo	return to the original tempo
cantabile	in a singing style
crescendo, cresc.	becoming louder
da capo, D.C.	from the beginning
D.C. al fine	repeat from the beginning and end at *Fine*
dal segno, D.S. 𝄋	from the sign
decrescendo, decresc.	becoming softer
diminuendo, dim.	becoming softer
dolce	sweetly, gentle
espressivio, espress.	expressive, with expression
fine	the end
forte, f	loud
fortissimo, ff	very loud
grazioso	gracefully
larghetto	fairly slow, not as slow as largo
largo	very slow
leggiero	light

©San Marco Publications 2022

lento	slow
maestoso	majestically
mano destra, m.d.	right hand
mano sinistra, m.s.	left hand
marcato	play marked or stressed
mezzo forte, mf	moderately loud
mezzo piano, mp	moderately soft
moderato	at a moderate tempo
molto	much, very
ottava, 8va	the interval of an octave
pedale, ped	pedal
pianissimo, pp	very soft
piano, p	soft
poco	little
prestissimo	as fast as possible
presto	very fast
rallentando, rall.	slowing down
ritardando, rit.	slowing down gradually
rubato	flexible tempo with slight variations of speed to enhance musical expression.
spiritoso	spirited
staccato	play short and detached
tempo	speed at which music is performed
Tempo Primo, Tempo I	return to the original tempo
tranquillo	tranquil, quiet
vivace	lively, brisk

Signs

 accent - a stressed note

 **common time** - symbol for 4/4

 **crescendo** - becoming louder

decrescendo - becoming softer

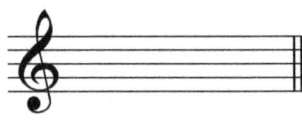 **double bar line** - the end of a piece

 **fermata** - hold note or rest longer than written value

 **slur** - play the notes smoothly (legato)

staccato - play short and detached

 **tie** - hold for the combined value of the tied notes

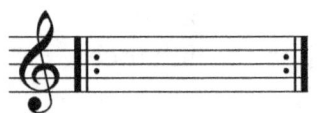 **repeat marks** - at the second sign go back to the first sign and repeat the music from there. The first sign is left out if the music is repeated from the beginning.

 **tenuto mark** - when placed over or under a note, hold it for its full value.

 **pedal symbol** - press/release the right pedal.

dal segno, D.S. - from the sign.

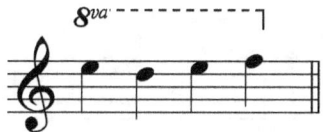 **8va** - play one octave higher than written pitch.

 **8va** - play one octave lower than written pitch.

 down bow - on a string instrument, play the note by drawing the bow downward.

 up bow - on a string instrument, play the note by drawing the bow upward.

, **breath mark** - take a breath or a small break

Exam

⑤ 1. Name the following notes.

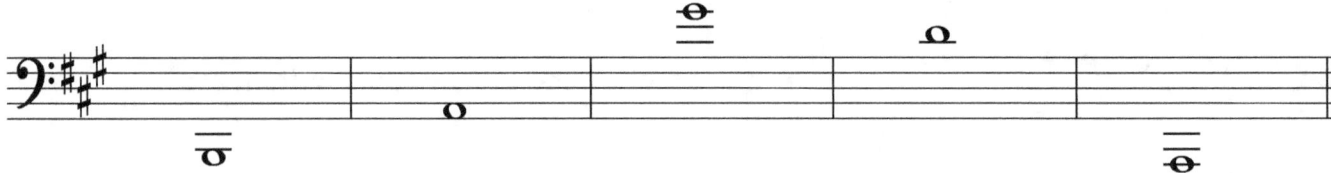

_____ _____ _____ _____ _____

⑤ 2. Name the following as chromatic half step (CHS), diatonic half step (DHS), or whole step (WS).

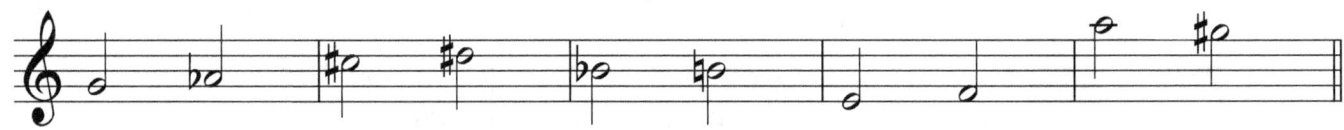

_____ _____ _____ _____ _____

⑩ 3. Write the following scales in quarter notes ascending and descending using the correct key signature for each. Label the dominant (D), subtonic (ST) and leading tones (LT).

E major

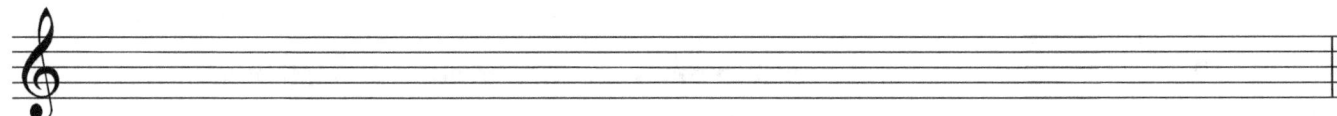

E major's parallel minor, harmonic form

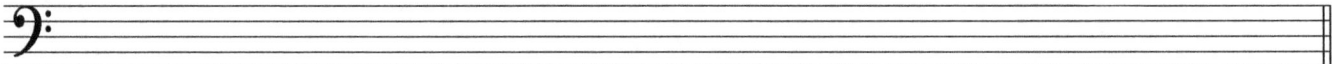

F minor, melodic form

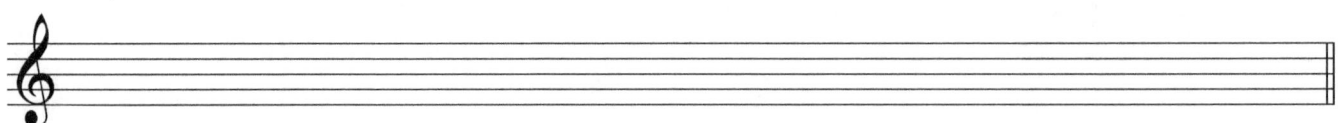

F minor's relative major

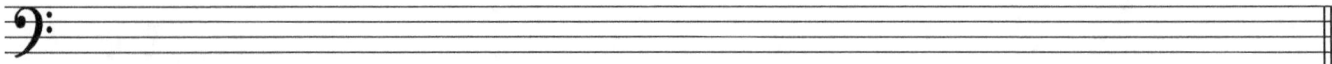

B minor, natural form

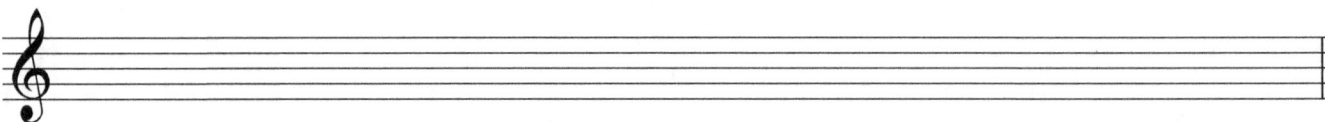

4. Name the following intervals.

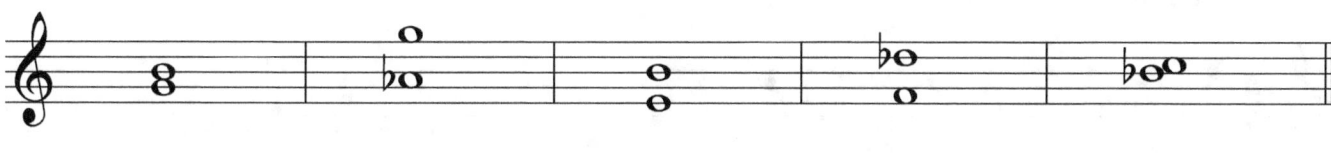

_____ _____ _____ _____ _____

5. Write the following intervals above the given notes.

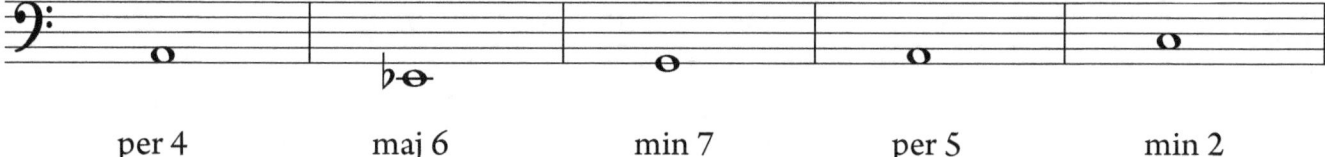

per 4   maj 6   min 7   per 5   min 2

6. Complete the following measures with rests under the brackets.

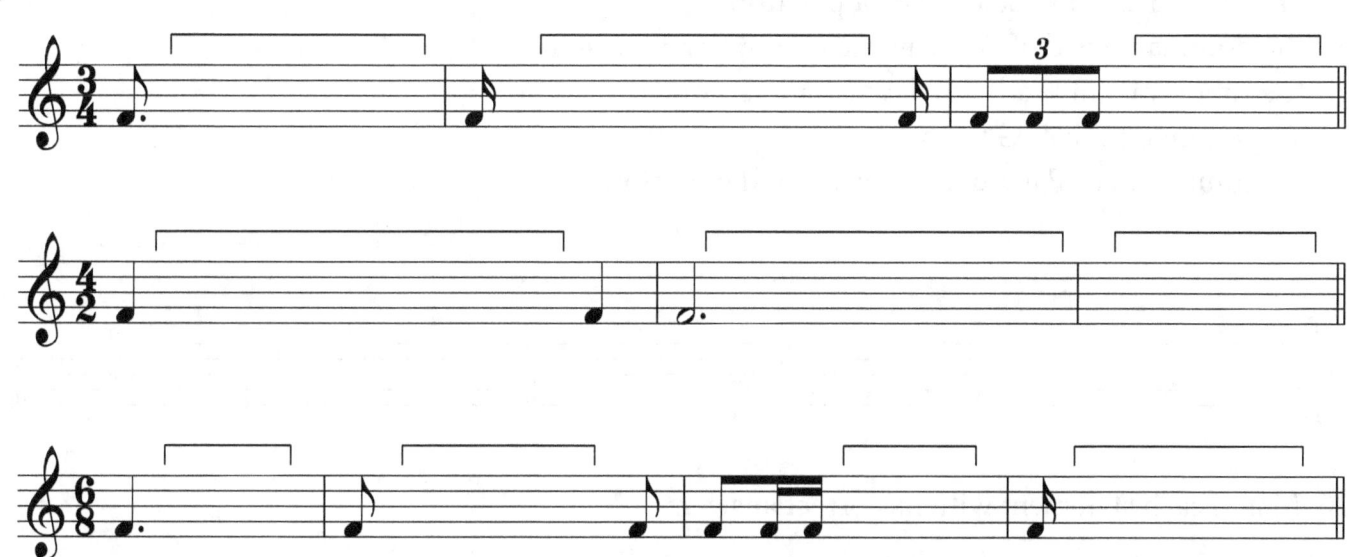

7. Name the key of the following melody. Transpose it down one octave into the bass clef.

key: _____

8. Name the key of the following melody. Compose an answer phrase to the given question phrase.

key: _____

9. Write the following chords using key signatures for each.

   i. the tonic triad of E major in root position
   ii. the dominant triad of D harmonic minor, first inversion
   iii. the subdominant triad of B flat major in second inversion
   iv. the dominant 7th of G major
   v. the tonic triad of F natural minor, second inversion

   i.   ii.   iii.   iv.   v.

10. Match each statement with its correct answer.

_____ Composer of "The Wizard of Oz"	a) Dorothy
_____ "Der Hölle Rache kocht in meinem Herzen"	b) "Over the Rainbow"
_____ Oratorio by Handel	c) Singspiel
_____ Opera by Mozart	d) Hallelujah Chorus
_____ Virtuoso female singer	e) Messiah
_____ Sings "Over the Rainbow"	f) The Magic Flute
_____ German born English composer	g) Handel
_____ Uses word painting	h) Queen of the Night aria
_____ Song in AABA form	i) Harold Arlen
_____ Name for German comic opera	j) Coloratura soprano

11. Define the following terms.

andantino _____

larghetto _____

rubato _____

largo _____

mano destra _____

poco _____

lento _____

pedale _____

spiritoso _____

marcato _____

prestissimo _____

tranquillo _____

dolce _____

leggiero _____

molto _____

espressivo _____

vivace _____

fine _____

marcato _____

adagio _____

12. Analyze the following musical excerpt by answering the questions.

Muzio Clementi
1752-1832

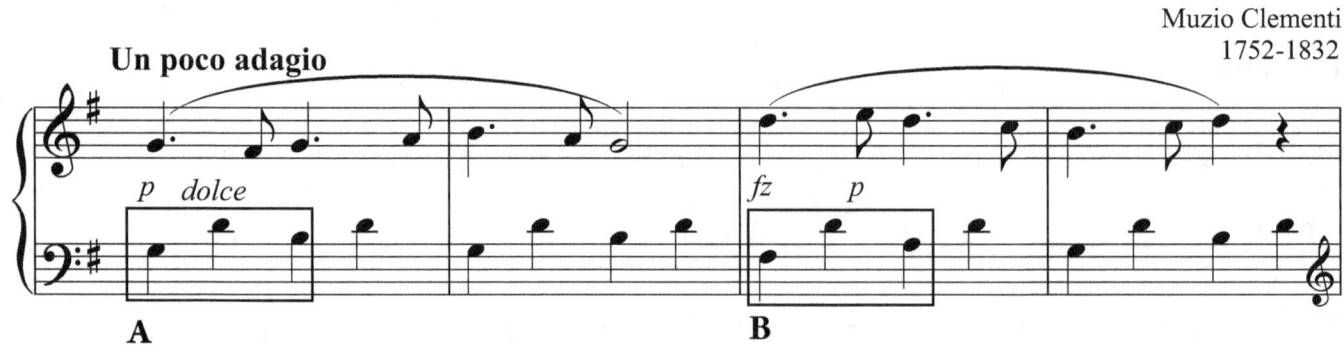

1. What is the key of this piece? _____

2. Write the time signature on the score.

3. Define **dolce** _____

4. Define **Un poco adagio** _____

5. Label the two phrases as: a - a¹ or a - b.

6. For the triad at A, name the: Root: _____ Quality: _____ Position: _____

7. For the triad at B, name the: Root: _____ Quality: _____ Position: _____

8. Find a chromatic half step in the score. Circle it and label it: CHS.

9. Find and circle a G major scale on the score. Label it: G major.

10. Name the highest note in this piece. _____

www.ingramcontent.com/pod-product-compliance
Lightning Source LLC
Chambersburg PA
CBHW081621100526
44590CB00021B/3547